mom's
NEEDS,
dad's
NEEDS

Other books by Willard F. Harley, Jr.

Fall in Love, Stay in Love
His Needs, Her Needs
Love Busters
Five Steps to Romantic Love
I Cherish You
The One
Surviving an Affair

mom's NEEDS, dad's NEEDS

keeping romance alive even
after the kids arrive

Willard F. Harley, Jr.

Revell
Grand Rapids, Michigan

© 2003 by Willard F. Harley, Jr.

Published by Fleming H. Revell
a division of Baker Publishing Group
P.O. Box 6287, Grand Rapids, MI 49516-6287

Paperback edition published 2005
ISBN 0-8007-3101-8

Previously published under the title *His Needs, Her Needs for Parents*

Second printing, September 2005

Printed in the United States of America

The Library of Congress Cataloging-in-Publication Data for the hardcover edition is on file at the Library of Congress, Washington, D.C.

ISBN 0-8007-1833-X (cloth)
ISBN 0-8007-5936-2 (intl. pbk.)

Scripture is taken from the HOLY BIBLE, NEW INTERNATIONAL VERSION®. NIV®. Copyright © 1973, 1978, 1984 by International Bible Society. Used by permission of Zondervan. All rights reserved.

Contents

1

And Then There Were Three
Are Children a Threat to Your Marriage?

Romantic movies are all alike. A man and woman are thrown together by unusual circumstances. They fall madly in love despite overwhelming adversity. And in the end they run into each other's arms to kiss under a moonlit sky before walking hand in hand toward a bright future together.

But these movies don't lend themselves very well to romantic sequels. Imagine what one might be like. The couple would now be married with three children. Instead of moonlit walks, they'd be helping the six-year-old with a school project, potty training the three-year-old, and trying to settle down the crying baby. And instead of running into each other's arms, they'd be running around the house, trying to get everything ready for another busy day of work, school, and household tasks. Talk about overwhelming adversity! At the end of the day our couple would collapse into bed, completely exhausted. How could even the best director make *that* look romantic?

There's good reason why they don't make many sequels to romantic movies.

Most couples tie the knot because they are in love. They want to be lovers for life, so they marry. And they assume that nothing will keep them from caring for each other—least of all, children.

But unlike the movies, where the final credits pop on the screen after the wedding, real-life couples have to handle the ups and downs of marriage. And once children arrive, they face even more challenges. The presence of children distracts them from their original objective—to care for each other. Caring for the children suddenly becomes their highest priority. With less time and energy to care for each other, their love gradually fades, and the once starry-eyed couple forgets why they ever married.

Sound familiar? If so, you're not alone. Many couples lose their love for each other after children arrive. I've counseled thousands of these couples, who usually are on the brink of divorce. And I tell them all the same thing: Your marriage can be saved only if you make caring for each other your top priority. And the best way to do this is by spending time together—away from your children.

> My advice for parents is simple. If you want to be good parents, you need to care for each other first.

You may question that advice at first. After all, natural instincts tell us that children are more important than anything else in life. And doesn't it sound selfish to take time away from them so that we can be alone with our spouse?

Children do need very special love and care, and responsible parents must give them the time and attention they need. But children desperately need something else too—parents who love each other and stay married. Numerous studies have shown that children of happily married parents are healthier, mentally and physically, than children of divorced parents. They usually become better educated and more successful later in life, and they are less likely to become criminals or to suffer as victims of domestic violence.

So my advice for parents is simple. If you want to be good parents, you must care for each other first. Your children's future depends on it.

What's at Stake?

If I offered you a million dollars to stay in love for ten years after your children arrived, how would you earn the money?

You might have a good idea of what it takes to keep love alive, if you can remember how your love was first created. When you were dating, you were affectionate with each other; you talked to each other the way lovers talk; you spent your recreational time together; and you were attracted to each other sexually. So to keep your love alive you'd probably create enough privacy and time to do all the things that kept you emotionally connected while dating. And after ten years, I'd owe you a million dollars.

Well, I can't pay you to stay in love, but there's actually something more valuable than money at stake when it comes to your marriage. If you can stay happily married, your children will benefit from living in a stable home and seeing a healthy model for marriage. And they'll be spared the extreme pain and confusion of witnessing a divorce.

CONSIDER THIS

If you're not in love with each other after ten years, you may lose more than a million dollars over the course of your lifetime. Without love, everything will be more difficult and less rewarding for you. And if you divorce, you'll experience legal fees, lost income, lost savings and investments, lost health, lost support from an extended family, and more—all of which can easily exceed a million dollars!

In case after case, children report extraordinary trauma during and after their parents' divorce. Just prior to divorce, parents often try to tell their children why they feel the ordeal is necessary. They explain that they simply don't love each other anymore or that their fighting is creating a bad environment for their children.

But children usually don't want to solve these problems through divorce. They just want their parents to love each other again and stop fighting. And that's exactly what parents should do. They should do whatever it takes to love each other—for their children's sake.

I've helped thousands of couples avoid divorce by restoring their love for each other. And many of those couples did it for their children. They knew that their children needed them to stay together. And that's enough incentive for most couples to follow my plan. But there's another reason that's just as important.

> Parents should do whatever it takes to love each other for their children's sake.

Is it a good idea to stay married for the sake of your children? Absolutely! Should you avoid fights if you stay together? Definitely! But why just stay married and avoid fights? Why not also be in love? You'll find that if you are in love, you'll want to stay married and avoid fights. And best of all, your lives will be far more fulfilling when you are in love.

Prioritize Love

So how can you guarantee the lifelong marriage your children need you to have? How can you stay in love even while raising a busy family? The answer is remarkably simple. In most cases, it doesn't require entirely new skills. All it takes is going back to what created your love in the first place—caring for each other just like you did while dating.

Unfortunately, most parents don't make time to care for each other. When children arrive, careers and domestic responsibilities shift into high gear. Parents come home from a challenging day at work to find household responsibilities and children who need their attention. By the time they get to bed, they are so tired that they dread the thought of more responsibilities—those of caring for each other.

On top of all that, parents tend to feel overwhelmed. So they seek refuge away from their children—where they can finally relax. Since parents are rarely together without their children, they end up creating recreational interests that do not include each other. And they spend their most enjoyable moments apart.

Have you fallen into these habits? Do your children, career, and household responsibilities require so much time that you have none left for each other? If so, you are failing to care for each other—and your children. When you stop giving each other the care you need, you start losing your love for each other. And when that's lost, you risk losing your marriage, something your children desperately need. Children suffer when their parents divorce. And they thrive when Mom and Dad make their care for each other a top priority. But kids can't set priorities for their parents. And they can't stop their parents from neglecting each other after they're born. So it's up to you to keep your priorities straight.

> Children suffer when their parents divorce. And they thrive when mom and dad make their care for each other a top priority.

Give Love Time

My wife, Joyce, and I value our children above life itself. Jennifer and Steven are our greatest treasures and achievements. They now have children of their own and feel the same way about them.

You are probably just as protective and caring of your own children. But if that concern changes your priorities, making time with your children more important than time with your spouse, your marriage will be at risk. Because it takes time to be in love.

Most married couples never realize this crucial fact. They think chemistry will keep them together because they're soul mates. Or they think that a commitment to stay married will guarantee their success. While both of these factors are important, millions of couples have discovered that they don't prevent divorce. When spouses neglect each other, they usually lose both chemistry and commitment.

Fortunately, you and your spouse don't need to learn this lesson the hard way. If you care for each other, you'll be able to sustain your love almost effortlessly. But it does take time to provide that care, and it takes privacy. You can't do it with children running around your feet. You'll need to carve out time from your busy schedule for just the two of you—time for intimate conversations, heartfelt affection, passionate lovemaking, and pure relaxation. These things are what you needed from each other when you were first married, and you still need them today. Truth is, you have the time for everything that's important—including your children and your marriage—if you schedule it wisely. And the wisest part of your schedule will be the time you spend caring for your spouse.

If marriage and parenting leave you feeling overwhelmed, you're not alone. Most couples feel the way you do after children arrive. But don't make the mistake that leads most couples into a loveless marriage, letting the pressures of life destroy their romantic relationship. Instead, make caring for each other your top priority in spite of all the pressures you face.

Your children learn from the way you care or don't care for each other.

This book will give you the tools to achieve that valuable objective. And it will also give you tools to raise happy and successful children. In fact, you'll find that those two objectives go hand in hand. Doing what it takes to stay in love with each other will help your children grow up to be happy and successful. And raising children the right way will help you build a love that lasts a lifetime.

Your marriage may never be the subject of a big screen movie. But to your children, it's the most important love story they know. They watch and learn from the way you care—or don't care—for each other. They weren't around for the first production that showed you falling in love and marrying to be with each other for life. All they get to see is the sequel, how you try to sustain your love for each other as you face life's challenges—including them. Their future health and happiness, and yours, depend on that sequel being just as romantic as the first production.

PART *1*

ROMANTIC
RELATIONSHIPS 101

2

What's Love Got to Do with It?

Why Romance Matters

If you've just recently married, romance may be so fresh in your mind that the answer to the question I raise in this chapter title may be obvious to you. But if you have one or more children, romance may be such a distant memory that you wouldn't know where to begin in trying to answer it. You may be shaking your head right now, wondering what happened to the passion you and your spouse once shared so effortlessly.

Over the years, I've developed a good understanding of romantic relationships and what it takes to keep them alive, even after children arrive. But before we can look at specific parenting challenges, I'll need to explain some essential concepts that will be revisited later in the book. For those of you who've read my other books, much of the material in this first part, "Romantic Relationships 101," will sound familiar.

What Is a Romantic Relationship?

The subject of romance can be very confusing. And it's no wonder. There's very little sensible information available on the topic. In my twenty years of formal education, including a specialization in psychology, not a single course on romance was available to me. Most material comes from popular books and magazines that do little to illuminate the reader.

Confusion about romance is partly due to the radically different perspectives of men and women. Men tend to think of romance one way, and women tend to think of it another way. So when the word is used, men and women have entirely different expectations. Since romance is something they share together, it's no surprise that many are confused.

I'd like to clear up any confusion you may have on this subject by giving my own definition of a romantic relationship. *A romantic relationship consists of two people in love who meet each other's emotional needs for intimacy.*

Some people who are not in love think they have a romantic relationship because they try to meet each other's intimate emotional needs. Others feel that only love is needed to define a romantic relationship. But if you give it a little thought, I think you'll agree with me—people are not in a truly romantic relationship unless they are in love *while* meeting each other's needs for intimacy.

The two parts of a romantic relationship: (1) two people in love who (2) meet each other's intimate emotional needs and depend on each other for their survival. You can't have one without the other—at least not for long. That's because meeting intimate emotional needs creates the feeling of love, and those who are in love with each other meet intimate emotional needs best.

But the interdependence of these two parts makes romantic relationships very fragile. When the feeling of love dies for either person, the romantic relationship temporarily ceases to exist. And even when both partners are in love, if one fails to meet the other's intimate emotional needs due to circumstances beyond his or her control, the romantic relationship temporarily ends.

I'm sure you've noticed how fragile your own romantic relationship is—if you still have one. You may find yourselves loving each other one day and hating each other the next. And you may be just as inconsistent at meeting each other's intimate emotional needs. If that's been your experience, you may question how long this can go on. Romantic relationships can be emotionally draining, and you may wonder if all the ups and downs are worth it. Is it just too much work? Maybe you've come to a point of despair, thinking you'll never have a romantic relationship with your spouse.

Well, I have good news for you. There's a way to keep your romantic relationship healthy and relatively effortless in spite of how fragile it can be. And there's a way to restore it again if it's been lost. That's what this book is all about.

But before we dive in too far, let's look at the definition of a romantic relationship more closely. It's important to understand its

SOUND FAMILIAR?

Becky let out a frustrated sigh as her husband, Jared, rushed out of the house, late for an "important meeting." *He didn't even kiss me good-bye.* He had been working late hours again, and she'd hardly had a decent conversation with him all week.

Was it just last weekend that he'd come home early to surprise her with special dinner plans? They'd left the kids with a baby-sitter and had a good time laughing, talking, and holding hands at the restaurant. But today Becky wasn't feeling so enamored. *How can we swing between happy couple and distant strangers in just a week?* she wondered.

two main concepts—love and intimate emotional needs—and how they affect each other.

What Is Love?

There are two kinds of love. The first kind of love is one of the essential ingredients in a romantic relationship; I call it **romantic love.** It's the feeling of being in love—finding someone emotionally irresistible.

I wanted to better understand romantic love, so I wrote one hundred questions I thought might have something to do with it. I gave those questions to several hundred people who told me they were in love and several hundred who told me they were not in love. I found that twenty of my questions were particularly discriminating—those in love consistently answered them one way, and those not in love answered the other way. I've used that twenty-item test to measure romantic love ever since.

Some of the questions in my test get at the very essence of how it feels to be in love:

Do you usually have a good feeling whenever you think about your partner?

Would you rather be with your partner than anyone else?

Do you enjoy telling your partner your deepest feelings and most private experiences?

Do you feel "chemistry" between you and your partner?

Does your partner bring out the best in you?

My test revealed the obvious—romantic love is a feeling of incredible attraction to someone of the opposite sex, and it's unmistakable for those who experience it.

But my test also helped me demonstrate another fact that's not so obvious to most people. As couples followed my plan for marital recovery, their scores would rise until they were in love again. And then, years later, when they took the test again, their scores would remain high. So I found that romantic love isn't a feeling couples must ultimately lose in marriage—it's a feeling they can experience for life. And I've proven that fact in my own marriage of forty years.

However, romantic love is not the only kind of love. There's a second type that is also very important. I call it **caring love** because it's a decision to care for someone—a willingness and effort to try to make someone happy.

> Romantic love isn't a feeling couples must ultimately lose in marriage—it's a feeling they can experience for life.

People can have caring love in many relationships. The love you have for your children is caring love. And you may also care for your parents and close friends. In fact, you may care for people you don't even know when you decide to invest time and resources with charitable organizations that help those people.

Although I haven't done it, I could develop a test for caring love—your willingness and effort to make your spouse happy. It would include questions about how concerned you are about your spouse's happiness and how you try to improve your spouse's quality of life. But a test of caring love wouldn't necessarily predict your marital success, because sometimes the way you care may not actually make your spouse happy.

For example, a husband may show his caring by purchasing jewelry for his wife. But what if his wife doesn't want jewelry—she craves some heart-to-heart conversation instead? If the husband is too busy to fill her need for conversation, his marriage will be headed for the rocks, no matter how much jewelry he gives her.

Some marriage counselors think your spouse just wants to know you care. But they're wrong. Knowing that you care isn't enough to sustain a romantic relationship. I've counseled hundreds of couples who care about each other but have still filed for divorce. Why? Because their care for each other has failed a crucial test—it doesn't meet intimate emotional needs.

I'll explain what those important needs are a little later in this chapter. But for now I simply want you to be aware of this fact: If your acts of care don't meet your spouse's intimate emotional needs, they won't sustain your romantic relationship. But if your care does effectively meet those needs, your spouse's feelings of romantic love will grow. In fact, your spouse's romantic love for you is a good test of whether or not your care actually meets his or her needs.

Unless a couple has caring love—they are willing to do what it takes to make each other happy—it's not likely that they will meet any of each other's needs, intimate or otherwise. So it's important that you and your spouse care for each other. But if you are to be in love, you must care in a very special way. You must meet each other's intimate emotional needs.

The Love Bank

Romantic love isn't something magical. And it's not some sort of mystical sign that you are eternal soul mates. It's actually an emotion your brain creates or eliminates based on certain experiences. It can be turned on and off with predictable certainty, which is why my job is possible. By understanding the factors that create and destroy emotions of romantic love, I show married couples how to rediscover lost love and keep it once it's been found.

To help my clients understand the predictability of love, I've invented the concept of the **Love Bank.**

There's a Love Bank inside each one of us. Every person we know has an account in our Love Bank, which keeps an emotional record of how they treat us. If a person makes us feel good, the figurative teller deposits some "love units" into his or her account. The better we feel, the more love units are deposited. But if that person makes us feel bad, our emotions withdraw love units from his or her account. And if we feel bad enough, it can be

> There's a Love Bank inside each one of us that keeps an emotional record of how people treat us.

like a bank robbery that wipes out the whole account. If withdrawals continue long after deposits have been exhausted, a Love Bank account can be overdrawn—it can be in the red.

Our Emotions Use Love Bank Balances to Motivate Us

The Love Bank serves a very important role in your life: It motivates you to be with people who treat you well and avoid those who hurt you. When someone's Love Bank balance is high, your emotions pull you toward that person. But when their balance is overdrawn, in the negative range, you have a feeling of repulsion and try to stay away.

These emotional reactions—attraction and repulsion—are not a matter of choice but are dictated by Love Bank balances. Try "choosing" to be attracted to those you associate with some of your worst experiences—it's almost impossible. Or try to feel repulsed by those associated with your best feelings. Not so easy, right? You can't decide whom you will like or dislike. It's the feelings you associate with them—whether they've made Love Bank deposits or withdrawals—that determine your emotional reactions.

So we like those with positive Love Bank balances and dislike those with negative balances. But if an account builds up to a certain threshold, a very special emotional reaction is triggered—romantic love. We no longer simply like the person. We are in love—feeling an incredible attraction to someone of the opposite sex.

If love units slowly collect over time, an account can eventually break through the romantic love threshold. But the threshold is more likely to be broken if love units are deposited quickly. As I will explain later in this chapter, the best way to make rapid deposits is to meet intimate emotional needs. When those needs are met, we feel so good that we fall in love.

Our emotions encourage us to spend time with those who have large Love Bank balances, because they make us feel good. But when someone's balance breaks through the romantic love threshold, our emotions make us *crave* time with him or her. That person has proven his or her ability to take especially good care of us, and our emotions want us to have as much of that care as possible. When we're together, the sun is shining and we feel fulfilled; and when apart, we feel like we've been hit by stormy weather. So the feeling of love usually draws us together for significant amounts of time, and it eventually encourages us to spend our entire lives together.

But our emotions give us more than just feelings of love. When they identify someone who makes us happy, they usually give us a strong dose of caring love. They do this by making it seem almost effortless to do what makes the one we love the happiest.

Have you ever noticed that when you are in love, you seem instinctively affectionate, conversant, and eager to make love? That's because your emotions want you to keep that person around, so they give you instincts to help you make that person happy, which, if effective, triggers his or her feeling of love for you.

The "look of love" not only communicates our feeling of love for someone but also reflects our instinct to do whatever it takes to make that person happy. And it's when you meet intimate emotional needs that you make someone the happiest.

What Goes Up Can Also Go Down

Wouldn't it be great if you could just fill up your spouse's Love Bank once and then coast happily through marriage? Unfortunately,

SOUND FAMILIAR?

Angie couldn't wait for Nathan to get home. Since they discovered she was pregnant last month, he had talked with her for hours about their baby, even calling her throughout the day to see how she was feeling. She loved him so much she could hardly wait to be with him again. But today she had a surprise for him and couldn't wait to see his reaction. She had planned a getaway weekend for the two of them, complete with tickets to see his favorite hockey team. She knew they would have a great time together!

what goes up can also go down, and Love Bank balances are no exception.

As you've probably discovered, the feeling of romantic love is very fragile. Love units have a way of vanishing and must be constantly replenished. It's as if the Love Bank leaks. That's why small deposits over a long period of time will not usually raise the balance over the romantic love threshold—they leak out almost as fast as they're deposited. It takes large deposits to fall in love, and those deposits must be made continuously to stay in love. If you stop meeting each other's intimate emotional needs, your Love Bank balance will fall below the romantic love threshold—you'll lose the feeling of love.

But failing to meet intimate emotional needs is not the only way to lose love. There's a more direct way. If you do something that makes your spouse miserable, love units don't just leak out of your Love Bank. They pour out. And most married couples seem to be born to make each other miserable. Selfish demands, disrespectful judgments, angry outbursts, dishonesty, annoying habits, and independent behavior—I call these Love Busters because they destroy love. And they are all very common in marriage. In chapter 5, I'll describe each of the six Love Busters and show how to prevent them from draining your Love Bank. But for now I simply want you to be aware of the fact that you drain your Love Banks when you make each other unhappy.

Whether you fail to meet each other's intimate emotional needs or you deliberately make each other unhappy, the result will be the same—you'll lose your love for each other. And when the feeling of love is lost, you'll also lose the instinct to make each other happy. What was once effortless will become awkward, even repulsive.

> When the feeling of love is lost, you'll also lose the instinct to make each other happy.

And instead of the look of love, you will have the look of apathy. Without love, your emotions will no longer encourage you to spend your lives together. They will encourage you to divorce, or at least try to get through life by ignoring each other.

Intimate Emotional Needs

As I mentioned earlier, my definition of a romantic relationship has two inseparable parts—(1) two people in love who (2) meet each other's emotional needs for intimacy. We've already discussed the first part of this definition, romantic love. So now we'll look at the second part—intimate emotional needs. Once you understand what these needs are, you can learn how to meet them for each other throughout your married life—especially when you have children.

What's an Emotional Need?

We all know about physical needs. Food, water, oxygen, warmth—these are essential to our survival, and with them our bodies thrive. Without them, we die.

But we also have other needs—emotional needs. When these needs are not met, we don't die, but some of us wish we would. An emotional need is a craving that, when satisfied, leaves us feeling happy and content. When it's unsatisfied, we feel unhappy and frustrated.

Most physical needs are also emotional needs. Physical deprivation leads to emotional craving, and physical satisfaction leads to emotional contentment. Food is a good example. When we're hungry, a physical need for food is accompanied by an emotional craving for food. The same is true of water.

But not every physical need is an emotional need. For example, we need oxygen but we don't have an emotional reaction every time the need isn't met. We can breathe helium instead of oxygen and feel okay right up to the moment we pass out. So oxygen is a physical need without an emotional component.

On the other hand, many emotional needs are *not* physical needs. What makes us feel good in life often has nothing to do with our physical well-being. In fact, there are many emotional needs that, when met, actually threaten our physical health. For example, we put our health at risk when we yield to the emotional craving for drugs or alcohol.

There are probably thousands of emotional needs—a need for birthday parties (or at least birthday presents), peanut butter sandwiches, *Monday Night Football*. . . I could go on and on. Whenever one of our emotional needs is met, we feel good, and when it's not met, we feel bad. Try telling a football fan that he can't watch the game this week, and you'll get a taste of how emotional needs affect people.

Not all emotional needs affect us with the same intensity. Some make us feel very good when met and very bad when unmet. Others have a small effect on us. In other words, if you meet some of your spouse's emotional needs, many love units will be deposited into your account in his or her Love Bank, while meeting others will deposit only a few.

The Most Important Emotional Needs

When a husband and wife come to me for help, their romantic relationship is usually a thing of the past. At the root of their desire to divorce lies the fact that they're no longer in love. In fact, many have actually come to hate each other. So my goal is to help them restore love and recreate the romantic relationship they once had. I show them how to avoid Love Bank withdrawals and how to make the largest Love Bank deposits. If they can raise their Love Bank accounts above the romantic love threshold, they will be in love with each other again, ending the risk of divorce.

When I first started using this approach to saving marriages, I didn't know what made people the happiest in marriage—I didn't know what a husband and wife could do for each other that would deposit the most love units. I had to ask hundreds of men and women this question: "What could your spouse do for you that would make you the happiest?"

As spouses explained to me what they wanted most in marriage, I classified their desires into categories of emotional needs. Almost all those I interviewed described one or more of the same ten emotional needs: affection, sexual fulfillment, conversation, recreational companionship, honesty and openness, physical attractiveness, financial support, domestic support, family commitment, and admiration.

But I made another discovery that helped me understand why husbands and wives tended *not* to meet each other's emotional needs. Whenever I asked couples to list their needs according to priority, men would list them one way and women a completely different way. Of the top ten emotional needs, the five listed as most important by men were usually the five least important for women, and vice versa.

Men tended to rank sexual fulfillment, recreational companionship, physical attractiveness, domestic support, and admiration as most important. Women, on the other hand, tended to rank affection, conversation, honesty and openness, financial support, and family commitment as most important.

Since the way men and women prioritize their most important emotional needs is usually so different, it's no wonder they have difficulty adjusting in marriage! A man can set out to meet his wife's needs, but he will fail miserably if he assumes her needs are the same as his. I've seen this simple error threaten many marriages. A husband

SOUND FAMILIAR?

James knew something was wrong with Renee. She was spending more time with the kids to avoid being around him. And she seemed to be angry with him, though he couldn't imagine why. He thought their relationship was great—they made love several times every week.

When he finally said something to Renee, he could hardly believe her response: "James, I don't really feel in love with you anymore! All we ever do together is have sex. When was the last time you talked with me for more than five minutes?"

and wife fail to meet each other's needs—not because they're selfish or uncaring, but because they are ignorant of what those needs are.

Granted, not every man or woman ranks emotional needs the way the average man and woman ranks their needs. In fact, there are many who rank at least one of their needs differently than the average man or woman. So even though I've discovered the most important emotional needs of average people, I don't know precisely what *your* needs are. That's why I encourage you to discover them and communicate them to each other.

Most people haven't given this much thought and wouldn't know where to begin if forced to make up a list of emotional needs. But it's important to understand what they are, not only for your sake, but also for the sake of your spouse. If he or she is to put time and energy into becoming an expert at meeting your needs, you'd better be sure you've identified the right ones!

I wrote *His Needs, Her Needs: Building an Affair-Proof Marriage* to help couples identify and learn to meet each other's most important emotional needs. I encourage you to read that book and complete the Emotional Needs Questionnaire if you haven't already done so.

But in this book, I will focus attention on only five of the ten important emotional needs. They are the four intimate emotional needs, and the need for family commitment. All five are so important to successful parenting that I want you to meet these needs for each other regardless of how you may rank them today.

Intimate Emotional Needs

Of the ten emotional needs I've identified as most important, four rise above the rest as crucial to a romantic relationship—affection, intimate conversation, recreational companionship, and sexual fulfillment. These are the intimate emotional needs, and they define a romantic relationship when met by lovers. The other six needs can be crucial in marriage, especially the need for family commitment. But without the intimate emotional needs being met, a romantic relationship simply ceases to exist.

As couples begin a family, they often neglect these intimate needs. The pressures of family life and shortage of time after children arrive tempt them to take shortcuts. The husband might think, *Why waste time talking so much—why not just have sex?* And the wife might think, *Why have sex so often—why not just spend our time talking to each other?*

But failure to meet each other's emotional needs is no shortcut—it's a path to romantic disaster. When a husband or wife's emotional needs are not met, they are less likely to meet them for each other in the future. The less willing he is to talk to her, the less willing she is to make love to him. And the less willing she is to make love, the less willing he is to talk to her. Cutting off affection and recreational companionship in marriage can have the same devastating effect.

The pressures of life, particularly the demands of raising children, make it a challenge to meet intimate needs. By now, you and your spouse may have drifted away from what made you lovers in the first place. But don't lose hope. You can restore your romantic relationship in spite of your new family—and for the benefit of your new family. If you keep reading, I'll show you how it's done.

> Failure to meet each other's needs is no shortcut—it's a path to romantic disaster.

3

Just between You and Me
Intimate Emotional Needs

Brenda and Jim were delighted when their little girl, Janelle, was born. They had both wanted children, and their first had finally arrived. But it was only a few months later that Jim's joy turned into alarm at the change that was taking place in his marriage—he and Brenda were hardly ever making love. At first he thought it would be a temporary problem, related to her delivery. But as time went by, he began to realize that the passion they once shared was gone.

He and Brenda used to spend their evenings and weekends going out dancing, taking long walks, cuddling while they watched videos or TV, or just relaxing while they listened to their favorite CDs. They would also go to concerts and sporting events together, but it wasn't so much the specific activities that were important to them—it was simply being alone with each other. And they almost always ended their evenings by making love.

Now it just wasn't practical to spend so much time together. Jim wanted his family to be financially secure, so he started working extra hours, and all of Brenda's free time was absorbed in the care of Janelle. And at the end of the day when Jim was expecting to make love, Brenda wasn't interested.

At first, Brenda was too excited about her new baby to notice the changes in her marriage. She appreciated Jim's willingness to work extra hours for their family and tried to be understanding when he came home feeling tired and cranky. But as the months passed by, she began to realize that he treated her differently. He didn't seem as interested in talking with her as he had been in the past. And he wasn't nearly as affectionate. He used to hug and kiss her dozens of times each night. But now he kept to himself after work. He would either sit watching TV or spend time in the garage working on some project. She knew that their relationship was going south very quickly but didn't know what to do about it. Whenever she tried to encourage Jim to spend more time with her and their daughter, he told her that he needed to have some time to himself.

By the time Janelle turned a year old, their marriage was in serious trouble—they were no longer in love.

Wired for Romance

Sometimes, even when both husband and wife do their best to create a happy family, everything seems to fall apart. And they wonder, *Why?*

The answer, in almost every case, is that their relationship has ceased to be romantic. When it comes to marriage, a romantic relationship is just about everything. With it, everything else falls into place—successful careers, financial security, robust health, and best of all, effective child training. Without it, just about everything you value is at risk, including your children.

A romantic relationship is absolutely compelling—we're wired for it. That's because the needs met in a romantic relationship—intimate conversation, recreational companionship, heartfelt affection, and sexual fulfillment—are among the most important needs you can meet for each other in marriage. And because they make such large Love Bank deposits, they shouldn't be met by anyone of the opposite sex outside of marriage, or you risk falling in love with the one who meets them.

That's an important reason why romantic relationships are crucial to marriage—your intimate emotional needs can't ethically be met any other way. You depend entirely on your spouse to meet all of them for you. When these needs are met, you are happy and fulfilled, and when they're not met, you feel sad and frustrated, just like Brenda and Jim.

> When it comes to marriage, a romantic relationship is just about everything.

Had Brenda and Jim realized how significant intimate emotional needs are, they would not have lost their love. But due to their ignorance, they let those needs go unmet after their daughter arrived, and as a result, their romantic relationship died.

How is your marriage doing? If you are no longer in a romantic relationship, it's not doing very well. Your feelings for each other will have grown stale because you've neglected each other's intimate emotional needs. But it's not too late. You can restore your love for each other by changing your priorities.

Intimate Conversation

Ordinary conversation is an emotional need that can be ethically met by anyone. Whenever you talk to someone in the course of a typical day, you may enjoy the conversation, but there is little risk of falling in love.

But intimate conversation is far different from ordinary conversation. If you talk with someone of the opposite sex about your deepest feelings and your most pervasive problems, you're engaged in the type of conversation that can bond you emotionally to that person. And since it can be so intense and enjoyable, it's easy to fall in love with that person. That's why I advise couples to limit their intimate conversation to each other.

Since intimate conversation can be so intense and enjoyable, it's easy to fall in love if your conversation is with someone of the opposite sex.

Intimate conversation tends to follow certain rules that I call the Friends of Good Conversation.

The first friend of good conversation is that your intimate conversation should help you investigate, inform, and understand each other. You should ask important questions, such as, How are you feeling? What are you thinking? What have you been doing? What are you planning? Then you should answer those questions honestly, ask for advice, and offer help regarding problems you both face. Such deep conversation provides an intimate understanding of each other that no one else knows.

The second friend of good conversation is to focus attention on topics of your greatest mutual interest. If necessary, become more educated in topics that your spouse seems interested in discussing so that you can become more interested in them yourself. In marriage, you are not born to be compatible—you create compatibility. And one of the best ways to create conversational compatibility is to gain background on topics that interest your spouse.

Good conversation should also be balanced so both people have an equal opportunity to talk. That's the third friend of good conversa-

SOUND FAMILIAR?

Leanne looked forward to her lunchtime conversations with Jack, a coworker who seemed to share her interests. He always listened and asked questions about her children and the happenings of her life. And she loved hearing him talk about his dreams for traveling the world. Some days, she even daydreamed about what it would be like to travel with him. *What am I thinking?* she'd realize with guilt. *I'm a married woman.*

tion. So never interrupt each other or talk so much that your spouse
has no opportunity to say anything. Intimate conversation is mutual
and bilateral. And if one of you tends to dominate the conversation,
it's not intimate—it's a speech.

The fourth and final friend of good conversation is to give each
other undivided attention. That means you should look at each other
and avoid any distractions. Don't try to have intimate conversation
while doing something else, like watching TV or getting some work
done. Eye contact is crucial. If your eyes wander around the room
while you're talking, it sends the message that something else is more
important. And when you talk intimately, nothing should be more
important than your spouse.

Unfortunately, even if you follow the friends of good conversation,
your conversation can still fail to be intimate if the enemies of good
conversation prevail. Enemies are what I call four destructive habits
that ruin good conversation.

The first enemy of good conversation is demands. Whenever you
tell your spouse what to do, instead of making a request, conversation
turns ugly. Control has no place in marriage, and whenever you make
a demand, you're attempting to control your spouse. Such an attempt
will result in a very defensive reaction from your spouse—a reaction
that will destroy your intimacy. You're not a sergeant and your spouse
isn't a private, so demands should never be part of your conversation.

The second enemy of good conversation is disrespect. If you think
you can "straighten out" your spouse, or if you find humor in making
fun of your spouse, think again. Intimacy makes people very vulnerable to disrespect, so don't say anything that's disrespectful. What
people need in an intimate relationship is admiration and support, not
criticism. So if your spouse's feelings are hurt by something you said,
apologize immediately. Chances are, what you said wasn't intended
to be disrespectful, but that's how it was perceived. Learn how to
avoid those perceptions of disrespect so that your conversation can
be free of land mines.

The third enemy of good conversation is anger. It goes without
saying that an angry outburst in the midst of an intimate conversa-

tion is devastating. Yet many couples I've counseled believe that their anger is an essential part of their very essence—and that if they don't express their anger, their spouse won't really understand them. One client told me that his anger was an expression of his creativity. Well, if that's true, he will have to learn to be creative by himself, because no one wants to be intimate with a monster.

We'll talk about demands, disrespect, and anger in greater detail in our next chapter. But for now, simply realize that these three habits will ruin any attempt at intimate conversation with your spouse.

The fourth enemy of good conversation is dwelling on mistakes of the past and present. Mistakes must be addressed somehow, but it's the "dwelling" on them that ruins intimate conversation. You may be thinking quite a bit about your spouse's mistakes, but if you talk about them as much as you're thinking about them, eventually you'll be talking to yourself.

These four enemies of good conversation drive people away from each other, making it less likely that they'll meet each other's need for intimate conversation in the future. People tend to avoid conversation when earlier attempts have been painful for them, so try to make your intimate conversations enjoyable for both of you.

You probably didn't have much difficulty engaging in intimate conversation during courtship, which was a time of information gathering. You wanted to discover each other's likes and dislikes, personal background, current interests, and plans for the future. And you tended to focus attention on each other's favorite topics.

Have you kept up that level of conversation since the wedding day? If you're like

---

Try This

Plan several one-hour dates where you simply practice the friends of good conversation. Find a sitter to stay with your children so you can be alone during these conversations. It might seem awkward at first, but after you've practiced for a while, you'll both look forward to these intimate conversations.

most couples, probably not. After children arrive, many women find that the man who used to spend hours talking with her now seems to have lost all interest in conversation. He now spends his spare time watching television or reading. And instead of balanced conversations, he either does all of the talking or doesn't talk at all. Undivided attention becomes a thing of the past—multitasking has taken its place.

But if your need for intimate conversation was fulfilled during courtship, you also expect it to be met after marriage. And you will be very frustrated if it is not met. But if it goes on for long, you'll be more than just frustrated—you'll no longer be in love. If you and your spouse are not meeting the need for intimate conversation, your relationship fails the romance test. And it also makes you vulnerable to having an affair with someone who does meet it. Don't let that happen. Apply the friends of good conversation and avoid the enemies whenever you take time to talk to each other.

Recreational Companionship

Recreational activities provide pure enjoyment; they give you something to look forward to after you complete all your responsibilities. And that's why they're an extremely important part of a romantic relationship—they make Love Bank deposits seem almost effortless. When a couple is in a romantic relationship, they are always each other's favorite recreational companions.

Before you were married, you probably planned your dates around recreational activities. You wanted to be certain that you were both enjoying yourselves when you were together, so you chose activities that would make that possible. You may not have known it at the time, but if you hadn't spent your recreational time with each other, you probably wouldn't have created the romantic relationship that led to marriage.

While dating, some couples do whatever the one with the greatest need for recreational companionship wants to do. That's what happened to Joyce and me. She was willing to join me in all of the recreational activities I liked the most—right up to the day we were married. But after marriage, she announced that she would only be joining me in activities that she also enjoyed. And it turned out that we shared very few recreational interests.

How would you solve this problem? Many couples make a crucial mistake—they go their separate ways. He joins his friends in recreational activities he enjoys and leaves his wife to find her own recreational companions. But that's a formula for marital disaster. If you aren't together when you're enjoying yourselves the most, you're squandering an opportunity to make crucial Love Bank deposits. And if someone else of the opposite sex joins you in your favorite recreational activities, you risk falling in love with that person.

> If you're spending your most enjoyable time apart from each other, you're not in a romantic relationship.

Fortunately, Joyce and I took the path that led to marital fulfillment. We decided to exchange activities that I alone enjoyed for new activities that we both enjoyed. We remained each other's favorite recreational companions after marriage, even though most of our recreational activities changed.

If you're spending your most enjoyable time apart from each other, you're not in a romantic relationship. But your problem may have been created out of ignorance. Many couples have been led to believe that men need to participate in certain activities that women can-

SOUND FAMILIAR?

Mark was barely in the door before his wife, Jane, was on her way out. He'd just returned from a Saturday afternoon of bowling and was in a good mood after reaching his personal best score. Now it was his turn to watch the kids while Jane went to see a movie with her girlfriends. "I won't be too late," Jane called as she walked toward the garage, "unless we decide to have coffee together afterwards."

not enjoy and vice versa. So instead of discovering activities to enjoy together, you decided to part company and find like-minded friends. Now you find yourselves looking forward to being apart because that's when you have the most fun.

The solution is simple—don't engage in recreational activities that you can't enjoy together. Instead, start searching for activities that are mutually enjoyable. This may sound unrealistic to you at first, but consider your Love Bank for a moment. Think of all the love units you could be depositing if your favorite recreational activities were with each other.

Right now, you may not know what those activities are, but if you were to discover them, as Joyce and I did, you'd no longer be squandering an opportunity to be in love with each other. What a waste if someone else got credit for all the love units you should receive during recreational activities. And if it were someone of the opposite sex, it would be downright dangerous.

The person who should get credit for all those love units is the one you should love the most—your spouse. And that's why I encourage you to be each other's favorite recreational companions. With a little trial and error, you'll discover mutually enjoyable activities that have been there all along. And they're one of the simplest ways to make large Love Bank deposits.

Try This

Make a list of all the recreational activities you would enjoy and then swap lists with your spouse. Pick the activities you would enjoy from each other's lists and then try them out one at a time. By the time you've found five activities you both enjoy, you won't have time for the rest of them!

Intimate Affection

We all need to know that someone cares for us, and people commonly express that care through affection. When you hug someone, you send them a message: "You're important to me, and I'll care for you." Hugs that are given to friends, relatives, children, pets, and even stuffed animals, can communicate a simple message of care.

But intimate affection goes much further. It communicates the care needed in a romantic relationship. Studies have shown that one of the quickest ways to make someone fall in love with you is to say you care for them and then prove it by the way you treat them. That's because intimate affection meets a very important emotional need, especially in women.

You may express intimate affection in many ways. A greeting card or an "I love you" note, a bouquet of flowers, hugs and holding hands, walks after dinner, back rubs, phone calls, and conversations with thoughtful and loving expressions—all can communicate intimate affection.

While almost everyone has a need for intimate affection, you've probably noticed that a husband's need is not usually as intense as the wife's. Husbands like to be told they are loved, but they don't generally have the craving for affection that their wives have. That's why I encourage every husband to create an "environment of intimate affection" by making affection with his wife a way of life.

So what does this affectionate husband look like?

An affectionate husband hugs and kisses his wife every morning while still in bed, usually for more than ten minutes, and tells her

SOUND FAMILIAR?

As she watched her son's soccer game, Linda noticed a couple standing hand in hand across the field. Every time their team scored, the husband hugged his wife and gave her an affectionate kiss. Linda couldn't help but feel jealous. *When was the last time Steve even tried to hold my hand?* she wondered to herself.

that he loves her. During their breakfast, he tells her he loves her again. He hugs and kisses her before he leaves for work. He calls her during the morning and again in the afternoon to ask how she is doing and to tell her that he loves her. Sometimes he invites her to go out for lunch, and sometimes they both meet at home for lunch so he can hug and kiss her and tell her that he loves her. After work, he calls before he leaves for home so that she knows when to expect him. When he arrives home, he gives her a hug and kiss and spends a few minutes talking to her about her day. He helps her with dinner and helps her clean up afterwards. He spends the evening with her, occasionally dancing to romantic music or giving her a back rub. When they go to bed, he usually hugs and kisses her while telling her that he loves her.

Does that description sound unreal? Well, I didn't come up with it by myself. It comes from countless women who told me what they want most from their husbands. And it also describes what goes on during a typical romantic relationship—it's what men tend to do when they are in love.

I encourage you to modify my description of an affectionate husband to fit your need for affection. Some of the behavior I've described may not impress you, and I may have left out some behaviors that you crave. So make up your own description so that your husband will know how to meet your need.

Granted, affection should come from the heart, and giving your husband a list of affectionate behaviors may seem contrived. But take my word for it: If you have a need for affection, you'll like what he does, even if it seems a little awkward at first. And once your husband gets into the habit of meeting your need for affection, it will be heartfelt and creative.

There's one more point I don't want you to miss. When both you and your husband meet all four intimate emotional needs, it won't take long before your love will be restored. And once you're in love again, your emotions will help you make affection just that much more heartfelt. Remember what I said about the "look of love"? It comes across loud and clear when lovers express their affection for each other.

But a couple must start somewhere when they've lost their romantic relationship. So I encourage the husband to use his wife's description of an affectionate husband as his guide. I show him how he can get into the habit of being affectionate by practicing these behaviors every day until they become almost effortless. At first, as he checks off each affectionate behavior every day, it seems very unnatural. But eventually, after about three months of practice, it becomes smooth and creative. By that time he's expressing his care from his heart and has become an affectionate husband.

> **Try This**
>
> Make a list of affectionate behaviors your wife would like you to learn. Then practice those habits every day until they become almost effortless. Among those habits, include going to bed fifteen minutes before you actually want to fall asleep just to cuddle with each other.

It takes repetition to form a habit. The more you practice a behavior, the easier it is to perform. But there's also another requirement. The behavior must be reasonably enjoyable if you want it to become a habit. If you try to practice a behavior that's unpleasant every time you do it, it will never become a stable habit. You'll jump at the first chance you have to avoid doing it.

So as you work through your list of affectionate behaviors every day, pay close attention to the ones that seem unpleasant, and replace them with more pleasant alternatives. Of course, the replacement behavior must be just as meaningful to your spouse. Otherwise it's not a habit worth forming.

Couples frequently ask me, "Who should take the initiative when it comes to affection?" My answer is very important because it clears up a crucial misunderstanding that often leads to deep resentment.

When a wife complains to her husband that he isn't being affectionate enough, he makes a serious mistake when he advises her, "If you want a hug, come on over and hug me." His suggestion misses the point. She doesn't just need a hug, she needs assurance that he cares for her. She needs him to hug her as an expression of his care. To expect her to initiate affection is like telling her to pick out his Valentine's Day card for her. What an insult!

Because most men don't have the same need for affection as their wives, they often fail to see its relevance, especially when their lives become very busy. But a romantic relationship can't exist without it. That's why it's so important for a husband to maintain an environment of affection for his wife, especially after children arrive. And that environment should reflect her unique interpretation of affection.

But just because affection isn't usually as important to men as it is to women doesn't mean that men don't need affection too. Affection is important to both men and women in a romantic relationship. So wives should also express their heartfelt affection. Of course, most wives have a much easier time being affectionate, because they usually have the strongest need.

Not surprisingly, intimate affection in a relationship outside of marriage can easily lead to an affair. It causes such large Love Bank deposits that when that need is met, the romantic love threshold is often breached. So your intimate affection should be reserved for each other and your children. Never tell someone of the opposite sex outside of your family how much they mean to you and how much you care for them. It's a formula for marital disaster.

If your marriage has lost its zip, it probably started to lose steam when you stopped giving each other intimate affection. But don't despair! You and your spouse can learn to restore affection to your relationship. And when you do, you'll find it much easier to meet the other three intimate emotional needs.

Sexual Fulfillment

What do you suppose would happen if you were to create the environment of intimate affection that I just described? With all that cuddling, I'll bet both of you would want to make love almost every day. Most of your sexual problems would become distant memories. Sex thrives in an environment of intimate affection.

The same is true of intimate conversation and recreational companionship (which we've already discussed). Couples who meet these emotional needs for each other find it much easier to have a fulfilling sexual relationship. That's because all four intimate emotional needs seem to hang together. When all four are met, each of them is much easier to meet. But when one of them is unmet, spouses struggle to meet the other three.

When intimate affection, intimate conversation, and recreational companionship disappear due to life's pressures, especially after children arrive, fulfilling sex usually disappears along with them. Yet most spouses, especially men, expect a passionate sexual relationship in marriage, even when they have no time for the other three needs.

When you married, you both promised to be faithful to each other for life. You agreed to be each other's only sexual partner "until death do us part." And you made this commitment because you trusted each other to meet your sexual needs by being sexually available and responsive. That makes you very dependent on each other for sex. You have no other ethical choices!

But if you'd been smart, your vows also would have included affection, intimate conversation, and recreational companionship. By promising to meet these other needs, you would have made it much easier to follow through on your promise to be each other's exclusive sexual partner. And you really are dependent on each other for sexual fulfillment. If either of you withholds sex from the other, you'll find yourselves very frustrated.

In most marriages, one spouse, usually the husband, has a greater need for sex than the other. This fact of life is often played up for amusement in television sitcoms, but in real life, it's not so funny. The husband gets frustrated when he doesn't get the sex he wants, and his frustration usually leads to fights, which makes her even less motivated to meet his need. So what can you do to avoid that very unhappy outcome? When your spouse stops meeting your need for sexual fulfillment—or any other intimate emotional need—how can you get what you need without violating your marriage vows?

I suggest something very similar to what I proposed regarding the need for intimate affection—get into the habit of having a fulfilling sexual relationship. As with affection, sex is something you can get into the habit of doing or get out of the habit of doing. It's much easier to make love if you're in the habit of meeting the needs of intimate affection, intimate conversation, and recreational companionship. But if you are not yet in the habit of meeting those needs, you should still be making love. So while you are still practicing behavior that will meet these other three needs, I recommend that you also practice behavior that will meet the need for sexual fulfillment.

> If either of you withholds sex from the other, you'll find yourselves very frustrated.

The more you practice any behavior, the quicker you'll get into the habit of doing it. So it's easier to get into the habit of making love if you do it every day, or at least when you spend a few hours together. In fact, I've found that couples with the most serious sexual problems and inhibitions seem to respond very well to an assignment that requires frequent lovemaking.

SOUND FAMILIAR?

Eric was starting to wonder why he'd ever agreed to having a baby. He barely got to spend any time alone with his wife, Stacy, anymore. And when they did have a few private moments, Stacy just wanted to talk. When he wanted to make love, he'd have to practically force her into it. And now she was using excuses to stay out of the bedroom until he'd fallen asleep.

But if the way you make love is unpleasant, practice itself will not get the job done—both of you must enjoy the experience. That means you both must respond to each other sexually every time you make love.

Many spouses, particularly women, don't understand their sexual response well enough to know how it is triggered. When they make love, they don't know how to become sexually aroused and experience a climax. If you are one of these people, I encourage you to read any one of the scores of books that are written to help improve lovemaking in marriage. I cover this topic in my book *His Needs, Her Needs: Building an Affair-Proof Marriage* (Revell, 2001) and its accompanying workbook, *Five Steps to Romantic Love* (Revell, 2002). Another very helpful book for women who have difficulty reaching a climax is *Women's Orgasm: A Guide to Sexual Satisfaction* (Warner Books, 1975) by Georgia Kline-Graber, R.N., and Benjamin Graber, M.D.

Men often make the mistake of demanding sex of their wives. The wives often comply but find the experience incredibly unpleasant. Instead of enjoying the experience, they suffer through it. Associating sex with pain instead of pleasure triggers an aversive reaction that can make them feel sick whenever sex is suggested. Eventually, the wife will do almost anything to avoid sex with her husband, even though it's one of his most important emotional needs. Her aversion becomes so strong that she just can't go through with it.

If you want to make it impossible for your spouse to meet your need for sexual fulfillment, demand it—make your spouse do it for you even if it's unpleasant. On the other hand, if you want your spouse to meet that need often, make sure she enjoys the experience every time. And if your spouse is to enjoy the experience, you must understand how she responds

---

Try This

Make love as often as the one with the greater need desires. But do it the way the one with the lesser need enjoys the most. By catering to the one with the lesser need, lovemaking will become more desirable to that person.

sexually and must guarantee that response whenever she makes love to you. The environment of affection goes a long way toward preparing most women for sex, but there are other details you must understand to make sex a good experience. If she explains to you what makes it enjoyable for her, and you follow her advice, she will usually make love to you as often as you would like.

Let me repeat what I've said earlier—when you are in love, all four of the intimate emotional needs are much easier to meet. So some wives have suggested that they wait until they're in love before they meet their husband's need for sexual fulfillment. But I advise both spouses to get into the habit of meeting each other's intimate emotional needs to trigger and maintain the feeling of love. And then, when they are both in love with each other, it will be just that much easier to continue meeting those needs.

Shortcuts Don't Work

As I mentioned before, men and women don't usually see romance the same way. Women tend to envision romance as acts of heartfelt affection and deep, fulfilling conversation. Men, on the other hand, tend to think of romance as having sex with a woman who is his favorite recreational companion. The truth is that romance is about all of those things, because they all fulfill intimate emotional needs. And to keep a romantic relationship alive, the expectations of both husband and wife should be met simultaneously.

But most couples strive for efficiency in life, especially after the children arrive. And romance is often its victim. In an effort to cut corners, men spend less time engaged in affection and intimate conversation with their wives, and women try to do with less sex and recreation with their husbands. Instead of creating a romantic relationship that is mutually fulfilling, they both eliminate the parts they feel are less important. And when that happens, romance comes to an abrupt end.

Quite frankly, both men and women crave all four of these needs —it's just that they're not prioritized the same. Women also want sexual fulfillment and recreational companionship, and men also want affection and intimate conversation. But they usually don't want it enough to get it at all costs. That's why it's easier for them to take shortcuts by forgoing intimate emotional needs that are not their highest priority.

> Most couples strive for efficiency, especially after children arrive. And romance is often its victim.

Maintaining romantic love isn't rocket science, but strangely enough, some of the smartest people on earth haven't figured this one out. They think romance is a mystery, something that comes and goes by pure chance. Or they think it's unsustainable—that within a year or two every romantic relationship is doomed to fade away.

They're wrong. The feeling of love is scientifically predictable. And it's not controlled by Cupid—it's controlled by the way a man and woman treat each other. When they fulfill each other's intimate emotional needs, their love for each other can last indefinitely. And when they try to take shortcuts, it dies away.

When you were married, you promised to care for each other in joy and in sorrow, in sickness and in health, in plenty and in want, as long as you both shall live. What that really meant is that you promised each other *romance* in spite of your circumstances. You committed to exclusively fulfill each other's most intimate emotional needs, and you didn't say "until children do us part."

If the romance in your marriage is slipping or is gone altogether, the clock is ticking. Sooner or later, one or both of you will crave romantic attention. Some try to find that fulfillment in an affair, and others simply by divorce. But you can avoid those disasters simply by keeping romance alive in your own marriage—and you do that by meeting each other's intimate emotional needs.

Love Takes Time

The Policy of Undivided Attention

When Joyce and I married, I thought I'd died and gone to heaven. Not only was I living with the love of my life, but I was also in an apartment that I only dreamed of having before I was married. Throughout my life as a college student, I was either living in a crowded dormitory room or sleeping in rooms that were provided to me as partial compensation for a job. Sometimes I even slept in my car.

And my car wasn't much. I bought it for fifty dollars because it was all I could afford. But marriage even improved my means of transportation. As a wedding gift, Joyce's mom and dad gave us an almost new Chevy Impala—a car that would actually start when you turned the key! My life certainly took a turn for the better on my wedding day.

During that first year, Joyce and I couldn't have been happier. We were faced with the responsibilities of completing our education and working to support ourselves, but nothing was more important than the time we had with each other. We were definitely in love and doing a terrific job meeting each other's intimate emotional needs.

We certainly had a great first year, but it wasn't our best year—the best was (and still is) yet to come. Over the years, we have not only sustained the love we had for each other but also built a lifestyle that both of us have thoroughly enjoyed. As we have grown together, the quality of our relationship continues to improve.

For many, however, the first year of marriage was their best, and love ran downhill from there. I think that's a tragedy, don't you? Yet many couples not only experience it, they're also led to expect it. Popular writers of marriage books often warn their readers that the passion of the first year will inevitably slip away, regardless of what's done to save it. One popular writer even considers a lifetime of marital passion to be a myth—an unrealistic expectation that leads many couples to divorce.

> Too many couples simply let their romantic relationship slip away, mistakenly thinking it's impossible to keep romance alive after marriage.

If my own marriage had not turned out to be as good as it is, I might have agreed with these writers—I wouldn't have known any better. But my own personal experience has proven to me that a marriage can be great when it starts and become even greater as the years go by—even when children enter the scene.

If these marriage "experts" had done what Joyce and I did to sustain our romantic relationship after the first year, they probably wouldn't find themselves in loveless, responsibility-driven relationships. But because they haven't created lasting love, they want to believe that no one can. Too many people simply let their romantic relationships slip away, mistakenly thinking that there's no use trying to preserve romance in marriage.

Just in Time

After seven months of marriage, Jeff felt that God couldn't have given him a more wonderful mate. And he was delighted with the recent discovery that their first child was on the way. But he was seeing red flags and didn't know what to do with them.

"We are very happy, and our unconditional love is, and always will be, the cord that holds us together," Jeff told me. "But Lori and I get so busy with our own schedules that we don't really have time for each other. And I don't think it's going to get any better when the baby is here."

Jeff's friends had suggested they get back to dating again by scheduling time to be with each other. But it wasn't as easy as it sounded. Now that they were married, it seemed awkward for them to plan a specific time together. Yet they both knew if they didn't take time to be with each other, they'd eventually feel like strangers.

Jeff's friends were right. Unless he and Lori set aside time to meet each other's intimate emotional needs, the romantic relationship that had propelled them into marriage would sputter and stall. They had to schedule a day and time to get together so they could meet those needs—a "date."

Before they married, dating had been an essential part of every day. Their love had been created with deliberate efforts to meet each other's needs. But after marriage Jeff and Lori were lulled into thinking that their "unconditional love" would carry them through. They didn't realize those efforts had to continue after the wedding vows if their romantic relationship was to survive.

Jeff saw the handwriting on the wall. He knew that they'd eventually become ships passing in the night if they continued on the path they were taking.

My advice to Jeff, and to you, is to waste no time in correcting the problem. The longer Jeff and Lori remain in the illusion that love never needs to be renewed, the harder it'll be to restore their romantic relationship after it's gone. Love Bank balances are relatively easy to maintain when they're high. But when they drop below the romantic love threshold, it's much more difficult to meet intimate emotional needs with enthusiasm. And when Love Bank balances have fallen into the negative range, it's about the last thing couples feel like doing for each other.

Your love is extremely fragile—totally dependent on your ability to keep Love Bank balances above the romantic love threshold.

And that takes time. You may feel as Jeff does, that dating seems awkward after marriage. And you also may feel that your busy schedules and the presence of children simply make formal dating impossible to arrange. But do you grasp the serious consequences of failure to meet each other's intimate emotional needs? Will you take time—scheduled time—to meet each other's needs?

The Policy of Undivided Attention

How did you and your spouse spend leisure time before you were married? Let me guess. If you were like most couples, you spent the majority of your leisure time together, and it was usually the most enjoyable part of your day. Spending time alone with each other was your highest priority, and you may have even canceled other plans when you had an opportunity to be together.

You probably tried to talk to each other every day too. If you couldn't physically be with each other, you talked on the telephone, sometimes for hours. And when you were together, you gave each other your undivided attention.

Did that all change after marriage? Did you, like Jeff and Lori, find yourselves drifting apart? And what about the days after your first child was born? Did that make matters even worse? Do you notice that you can be in the same room together and yet ignore each other because your attention is focused on your children? Or maybe you're not even in the same room very often.

One of the more difficult aspects of marriage counseling is scheduling time for it. Counselors often must work evenings and weekends because most couples won't give up work for their appointments. Then they must schedule around a host of evening and weekend activities that take a husband and wife in opposite directions.

But finding time for an appointment is easy compared to arranging time for the couple to be together for their first assignment. Many couples think a counselor will solve their problem with weekly conversations in his or her office. It doesn't occur to them that it's what they do after they leave the office that saves the marriage. To accomplish anything, they must schedule time together—time to give each other their undivided attention.

It's incredible how many couples have tried to talk me out of having them spend more time together. They try to convince me that it's impossible, or they argue that it's impractical. But in the end, they usually agree with me that without time for undivided attention, they can't recreate the love they once had.

And that's the point. How can you and your spouse meet each other's intimate emotional needs if you don't take time for undivided attention? You can't. And just like Jeff and Lori, you'll find that other, less important activities will crowd out your time. If you want to sustain and build your love for each other, you'll need to schedule time together.

To help Jeff and Lori meet each other's needs, I encouraged them to follow the **Policy of Undivided Attention:** *Give your spouse your undivided attention a minimum of fifteen hours each week, using the time to meet his or her needs for intimate affection, sexual fulfillment, intimate conversation, and recreational companionship.*

The Policy of Undivided Attention:

Give your spouse your undivided attention a minimum of 15 hours each week, using the time to meet his or her needs for intimate affection, intimate conversation, sexual fulfillment, and recreational companionship.

I encourage you to follow this policy too. It might sound impossible at first, but it's something every married couple can do. And it's something almost every dating couple does before they marry. Making time for undivided attention will help you avoid one of the most common mistakes in marriage—neglecting each other's intimate emotional needs.

There are three important parts to this rule—privacy, objectives, and amount.

Privacy

The time you plan to be together should not include children (who are awake), relatives, or friends. Establish privacy so that you are better able to give each other your undivided attention.
It's essential for you to spend some of your waking hours alone with your spouse almost every day. Without privacy, undivided attention is almost impossible, and without undivided attention, you can't adequately meet each other's intimate emotional needs.

Privacy is easier to achieve during the first year of marriage than at any other time. But most couples, like Jeff and Lori, don't use their privacy to establish habits that sustain their romantic relationship. Instead, they schedule each other out of their lives.

Some couples make privacy even more difficult by living with parents or in-laws to save money. And all parents face an added challenge to their privacy—the presence of children in the home. But regardless of circumstances, if you want your romantic relationship to thrive, you must learn to be together at least part of each day without relatives, friends, or children.

Try This

Find baby-sitting partners who will watch your children for one evening each week in exchange for you watching theirs on another evening.

If you're expecting your first child, learn to protect your privacy at all costs now; then it will be easier to continue after children arrive. And if you've already started your family, show your children how to build a healthy marriage by protecting your privacy. The habits and traditions you form today will set a precedent for years to come.

But don't be surprised if your commitment to privacy sometimes wavers because of your children. The instinct to be with your children whenever possible, especially when they are young, is so strong that it may weaken your resolve. You may think that your children don't really interfere with your privacy—that an evening with your children is privacy.

Of course, you realize you can't make love with children around. But the presence of children prevents much more than lovemaking. When children are present, they also interfere with intimate affection and intimate conversation that usually lead to lovemaking. Without the privacy to meet these other intimate emotional needs, you'll find that lovemaking suffers. And if your recreational companionship always includes your children, you'll be so restricted in what you find mutually enjoyable that you may be tempted to spend your most enjoyable leisure time apart.

What's true for children is especially true for friends and relatives—they shouldn't be with you during your time for undivided attention. This may mean that after everything has been scheduled, there's little time left for friends and relatives. If that's the case, you're probably too busy, but at least you won't be sacrificing your love for each other.

> ### Try This
>
> Taking a walk with your spouse every evening is a great way to spend time alone while also getting some of the exercise you need.

If you have children, you may be thinking that it's too late for privacy. You may feel that your lifestyle can't be changed. But don't despair. It's never too late to develop healthy habits. True, the task is more difficult after children arrive. But children also give you an added incentive to strengthen your marriage with privacy—their happiness depends on it.

Objectives

During the time you are together, create habits that will help you meet the emotional needs of intimate affection, sexual fulfillment, intimate conversation, and recreational companionship.

As I mentioned earlier, romance for most men includes sex and recreation, and for most women it involves intimate affection and intimate conversation. So imagine what happens when all four come together! Men and women alike call it romance and make massive

Love Bank deposits when meeting these needs for each other. That's why I recommend that you try to combine them all during your time together.

A wife often encourages her husband to meet her emotional needs for intimate affection and intimate conversation without making time to meet his needs for sex and recreational companionship. A husband, on the other hand, wants his wife to meet his needs for sexual fulfillment and recreational companionship but doesn't take time to meet her needs for intimate affection and intimate conversation. Neither strategy works very well.

A husband should never assume that just because he's in bed with his wife, sex is there for the taking. In many marriages, that mistake creates resentment and confusion. Most men eventually learn that if they spend the evening giving their wife their undivided attention, with intimate conversation and affection, sex becomes a very natural and mutually enjoyable way to end the evening.

But there are some women who don't see the connection either. They want their husbands to give them the most attention when there is no possibility for sex. In fact, knowing that affection and intimate conversation often lead a man to wanting sex, they try hardest to be affectionate when they are out in a crowd. This tactic can lead to just as much resentment in a man as nightly sexual "ambushes" create in a woman.

When all four needs are fulfilled in a single event, neither spouse feels resentment, and they both have their needs met. They enjoy their time together and are more likely to meet each other's needs in the future too. Take my word for it, fulfilling the four needs of intimate affection, intimate conversation, recreational companionship, and sexual fulfillment works best when they are met together.

Try This

Create a weekly baby-sitting night at your church or community center, where parents can drop off their children for two or three hours of free baby-sitting. Parents can take turns caring for all the children once a month.

Amount

The number of hours you schedule to be together each week for undivided attention should reflect your love for each other. If you and your spouse are in love, schedule fifteen hours each week to be together. But if one or both of you have fallen out of love, plan more time until marital satisfaction is achieved.

How much time do you need to sustain the feeling of love? Believe it or not, there really is an answer to this question, and it depends on the health of your marriage. If you're deeply in love with each other and find that your marital needs are being met, fifteen hours each week of undivided attention will probably sustain your love, if you use the time to meet each other's intimate emotional needs.

If your romantic relationship is still in great shape, you're probably giving each other all the time you need. In fact, you may be spending more than fifteen hours for undivided attention. But until you started reading this book, you may not have been aware of the connection between that weekly time and your feelings of love for each other. Now that you know, simply continue giving each other at least fifteen hours of undivided attention each week. That will keep your romantic relationship in great shape for the rest of your lives together.

But if you've lost your romantic relationship, you should schedule more time for undivided attention until your love has been restored. To help jump-start your romantic relationship, I suggest abandoning most other responsibilities so that you can spend twenty-five or thirty hours a week of undivided attention until you can meet each other's emotional needs almost effortlessly. In some cases I've even recommended a vacation together so a couple can give undivided attention around the clock.

The more time you spend meeting each other's intimate emotional needs, the more love units you'll deposit into each other's Love Bank. So if you want your Love Bank balances to break through the romantic love threshold quickly, spend as much time meeting each other's intimate emotional needs as you can. Then, when your romantic relationship is back on track again, fifteen hours a week should keep it healthy.

When I apply the fifteen-hour principle to marriages, I usually recommend that the time be evenly distributed throughout the week, two to three hours each day. When time is bunched up—all hours only on the weekend—good results are not as predictable. Spouses need to be emotionally reconnected on a daily basis to meet each other's most intimate emotional needs.

Where Will I Find the Time?

But where are we supposed to get fifteen hours? you may be thinking. *We barely have time to say good-bye in the morning before we get to work!*

Well, how does a workaholic businessman find time to have an affair? The man who couldn't be home for dinner because of his busy schedule is suddenly able to fit in a midafternoon rendezvous three times a week! How does he get his work done?

The answer, of course, is that he had the time all along. It's simply a matter of priorities. He could just as easily have spent the time with his wife. Then they would have been in love with each other. Instead, he's in love with someone else, and all because of his shortsighted schedule!

One reason I have so much difficulty motivating couples to spend time together is that they've forgotten how to meet each other's intimate emotional needs. At first, spending time with each other seems like a total waste. But when they use the time to recreate the romantic experiences that first nurtured their love, it eventually becomes their most enjoyable time of the week.

Don't neglect spending time together—it's vital to the security of your marriage and your children. It's more important than time spent doing anything else during the week, including time with your children and your job. And remember, fifteen hours is equivalent to a part-time job. It's not time you don't have; it's time you will use for something much less important if you don't use it for each other.

If you haven't been scheduling fifteen hours a week for undivided attention, let me remind you that you have about 168 total hours each week, and 110 of them are waking hours. If you prioritize your schedule, listing your most important activities first and least important last, you should eliminate the fifteen hours of least important activities to make room for your time together. Not a bad swap, is it?

Don't waste precious time hoping that somehow your relationship will improve. Take the first step to success by actually putting each other into your schedules. And once you're there, do whatever it takes to make it the best fifteen hours of your week.

Try This

Does it sound impossible to carve out fifteen hours from your current schedule? Plan a weekend away from work and family and use it to closely examine your schedules and priorities. Come back with a plan for creating a new schedule that leaves time for undivided attention.

It's on the Calendar

Time has a way of slipping away if you don't set it aside for important objectives. So unless you schedule that time, you simply won't get the job done. To help you plan your week with each other's emotional needs in mind, I encourage you to meet with your spouse at 3:30 Sunday afternoon to look over each other's schedule for the coming week. That's when you can make sure you've provided time for each other. And while you're at it, you can plan a little extra time just in case an emergency arises that interrupts your original plan.

I've included work sheets to help you plan your time together and keep a record of how the time was spent. The Time for Undivided Attention work sheet, found in Appendix B, introduces topics that I want you both to consider when planning your time and then later evaluating it.

Use the Planned Time Together part of the work sheet when you first schedule your fifteen hours. Then complete the Actual Time Together part throughout the week after each date is completed. On the following Sunday afternoon, when you are scheduling time for the next week, you can evaluate how the last week actually turned out.

The Time for Undivided Attention graph, found in appendix C, provides you a record of how many hours you actually spend each week giving each other undivided attention. I encourage you to put this graph in a prominent place where you can see if you're achieving your goal.

Try This

Keep your Time for Undivided Attention Graph in a place where your children will see it. This will help them understand why you can't be with them part of each week, and it will also teach them how to keep romance in their own marriages someday.

Your dates don't have to be exactly what you did before marriage. In fact, you may be able to meet each other's intimate emotional needs without actually going out. But when Joyce and I were first married, our evenings at home often turned into personal projects that took our attention away from each other. We had to go out to give each other the attention we needed.

Even if you schedule time together, you may find that the time you spend on dates doesn't meet your needs the way it did before marriage. If that's the case, try to rediscover what you actually did when you went on a date. You were probably very affectionate with each other, you probably talked together for hours, and you probably spent all of your recreational time together.

One couple I counseled found that their sexual interest in each other was completely restored by driving their car to a secluded and scenic spot where they had parked while dating. Their intimate conversation, while hugging, kissing, and listening to romantic music on the radio, was the trigger that was missing. Eventually, they were able to recreate the same experience at home without actually going for a drive. But if you want to try this yourselves, you may need to trade in your car with bucket seats for one with a front-bench seat! Dancing together accomplishes the same objectives as parking for many couples. Being in each other's arms with a favorite musical background can be very romantic. And it's something you can do going out or staying at home.

Cuddling while watching TV also can be an effective way to meet each other's intimate emotional needs. But make sure you are more interested in each other than whatever happens to be on the screen. You won't make any Love Bank deposits if you watch the commercials more closely than you watch your spouse.

> Remember, the most important gift you can give your children is the gift of your love for each other.

Even if you are now overwhelmed with the responsibility of raising children who seem to soak up every spare minute you have, it's still not impossible to give your spouse time for undivided attention. Remember, the most important gift you can give your children is the gift of your love for each other. And that love can be maintained only if you take time to meet each other's intimate emotional needs. So start scheduling time together today, before even more obligations fill up your calendar.

Which brings me to a very common problem in marriage: career pressures that make time together seem impossible to schedule. As you will see in my next illustration, the Policy of Undivided Attention can be a big help in making sure that your career doesn't interfere with your romantic relationship.

A Job That Broke the Bank

Like many other women, Danielle admired ambitious men, and Todd was one of the most ambitious she had ever known.

Though he worked his way through college by taking two jobs, he had outstanding grades. And he was so well organized that, in spite of his busy schedule, he made a point of seeing her almost every day.

But after their marriage, his career took off, and Danielle was squeezed out of his schedule. When she complained about how little time they had together, he would explain how important this phase of his career was, and how he would have more time for her and his family in a few years.

Ten years and three children later, nothing had changed. Todd was an absentee husband and father. At a point of desperation, Danielle made an appointment, without Todd, for my advice. During the session, she confessed that she'd fallen in love with another man and wouldn't be all that disappointed if her marriage ended in divorce.

Todd rarely discussed his work schedule with Danielle. And if he had, he wouldn't have had her agreement.

But did Danielle have a right to interfere with his career opportunities? She would if they wanted to recreate a romantic relationship. Unfortunately, by the time Danielle got to me, she didn't want Todd home at all. The time when she wanted his companionship had passed, and unless he included her in his schedule soon, he would lose her entirely.

Todd had made two crucial mistakes in his marriage. His first mistake was making career decisions without considering Danielle's interests and feelings. But his second mistake was making career decisions that prevented him from meeting her intimate emotional needs. And his account in her Love Bank was extremely overdrawn.

The needs that were unmet by Todd were met by Danielle's friend who willingly gave her his time and attention. That's why she fell in love with him. But I explained to her that she could have the same love for her husband if he met the same emotional needs. She was willing to give her marriage one more chance and agreed to inform her husband about her affair.

Todd Finds Time for Love

Three days later, Todd came to see me in a panic. "What can I do to save my marriage?"

I explained to Todd how his schedule had prevented him from meeting Danielle's intimate emotional needs. Without his undivided attention, Danielle's Love Bank had slowly but surely drained completely empty, and someone else had filled the void.

Todd was stuck in a schedule that was too busy to give Danielle his undivided attention. He had gone down a path where so many decisions had been made without the Policy of Undivided Attention that backtracking seemed almost impossible. He worked long hours to be successful at what he did, and his responsibilities sometimes required travel for a week or more. Missing those business contacts might jeopardize everything he had worked so hard to accomplish, especially a promotion that was on the line.

So how could he cut back and still get the job done? If Todd had tried to get out of his commitments slowly, Danielle wouldn't have been around long enough for him to complete the changes. And if he didn't take the time to meet her emotional needs immediately, her love for her friend would have overwhelmed her. Todd had to make changes fast if their marriage was to survive.

> It's sad that it takes an affair to get some couples moving.

Quite frankly, it's sad that it takes an affair or the threat of an affair to get some couples moving. It would have been much less painful for both Todd and Danielle if she had not fallen in love with another man. And it was a tragedy that would hang over their family for years to come. But it certainly put their marriage on Todd's front burner.

Todd agreed that if he didn't put Danielle's interests first, he would lose something much more important than his career. He also agreed that the most important time he could spend every week was time giving her his undivided attention. And it was not just for her—it was also for him. He'd been working so hard that his own intimate emotional needs hadn't been met.

So he put his career on the line. If changing jobs, or even changing careers, was what it took to win Danielle back, he was willing to do it. And that willingness to put her above his work gave him the chance he needed to save his marriage.

Danielle was surprised and impressed by Todd's reaction to the problem. She had always felt that his career was more important to him than she was. But now he was telling her he would give up his career if that was what she wanted.

That's not really what she wanted at all. She simply wanted to be his highest priority. And she was willing to negotiate with him about the details of his career so that they could create a new lifestyle that enabled him to meet her intimate emotional needs.

Danielle was also impressed with the way he handled the revelation of her developing affair. She had been afraid to confront him about her growing feelings for another man, for fear he would divorce her on the spot and humiliate her in front of their children and her family. But he did the opposite. He never discussed with anyone else what she had told him, and her relationship with the "other man" had never progressed beyond her feelings—the man didn't even know she was in love with him.

She followed my advice by telling Todd who the man was, and she agreed to end her relationship with him. And then they went to work re-creating the romantic relationship they once had. They planned their time together first, and then they fit in all their other activities and responsibilities of the week. They also decided to be together whenever Todd took a business trip away

---

Try This

Schedule lunch dates with your spouse, enjoying privacy at home if your children are in school or day care. It's a great way to escape the pressures of work and parenting while meeting each other's intimate emotional needs.

from home. The Policy of Undivided Attention helped them dodge a bullet.

It's Worth a Try

So how do you and your spouse feel about each other's careers? If your work schedules don't leave time for fifteen hours of undivided attention each week, you'll need to rearrange your priorities. But I guarantee you that those changes will make you happier than you are now. Like Todd and Danielle, you'll fall in love with each other again.

Maybe your careers are under control, but you've filled your lives with other activities: spending time with friends, taking your children to one sporting activity after another, volunteering for community events—all noble activities. But if you just can't say no to these things, you *are* saying no to time with your spouse, and your Love Banks will drain dry.

Love takes time, and you'll need to make the Policy of Undivided Attention a way of life to keep your love alive. And since the alternatives are a loveless marriage or divorce, don't you think it's worth it?

Love Bankruptcy

When Love Busters Break the Bank

I remember an old *Star Trek* episode when Spock volunteered to be possessed by an alien presence. This temporary possession allowed the alien to communicate with Captain Kirk of the Starship Enterprise.

The alien's very first reaction on entering Spock's body was, "Oh, how lonely you must all feel."

In the alien world, every being was connected to one another through mental telepathy. Each one could feel what everyone else felt, and they were very emotionally bonded to one another. But as soon as the alien possessed Spock's body, it realized that humans are emotionally cut off from one another. And it viewed our state as incredibly isolated and lonely.

I was struck by the truth of that episode. Humans really are quite isolated from one another—we can't read each other's minds, and no one can understand just exactly how we feel. But our emotional isolation doesn't just make us lonely—it also makes us thoughtless.

We don't feel the pain we inflict on each other, so we hurt others without even thinking about it. If we were emotionally connected like the *Star Trek* aliens were, we'd be far less thoughtless. When we tried to gain at someone else's expense, we'd quickly discover that we hurt ourselves as well.

Thoughtlessness can really make a mess in marriage. When I introduced the Love Bank to you, I mentioned that there's more to romantic love than just meeting intimate emotional needs. Even if we make sizable Love Bank deposits, we can still wreck it all by making large withdrawals. And because we lack empathy, we tend to make those withdrawals with thoughtless mistakes. So if you and your spouse want to stay in love, you'll have to learn how to avoid those mistakes.

Do you remember your dating days? You probably tried to protect each other's feelings as often as possible. In fact, if you hadn't been thoughtful then, you probably wouldn't have married. Couples who practice inconsiderate behavior withdraw so many love units that they don't usually date very long, let alone marry. While meeting intimate emotional needs created your romantic relationship, thoughtfulness protected it—at least while you were dating.

But since your children arrived, your thoughtfulness may have slipped a peg or two. With the new pressures you face, you may feel that you can't always worry about your spouse's feelings. Maybe you've found yourself getting what you want despite your spouse's objections. And maybe you fight with your spouse whenever you don't see eye to eye instead of trying to find a solution that works for both of you.

> Love Busters, if left unchecked, will make you the greatest source of each other's unhappiness.

If you've noticed thoughtlessness creeping into your marriage, it's time to confront Love Busters. By meeting each other's intimate emotional needs, you will be each other's greatest source of happiness. But if Love Busters are left unchecked, you will destroy the Love Bank balances you have built. You will become the greatest source of each other's unhappiness.

What Are Love Busters?

Whenever you do something that makes your spouse unhappy, you withdraw love units. A single careless act is bad enough. But if you repeatedly do something that makes your spouse unhappy, your Love Bank withdrawals can become serious enough to threaten your love for each other. I call habits that cause repeated withdrawals Love Busters because that's what they do—they destroy the feeling of love.

As I mentioned, lack of empathy is at the core of Love Busters—we don't feel the pain we inflict on each other. And that's what I always seem to battle when I encourage one spouse to avoid doing anything that would hurt the other spouse. Each spouse complains about how thoughtless the other one is, without much awareness of his or her own thoughtlessness.

For example, you may find it extremely rude that your spouse ignores you when you come home from work. But have you considered how rude it is to come home late without so much as a phone call? We don't feel the pain we cause others, so it's easy to focus on what bothers us and ignore what bothers others.

In marriage, there's a host of ways spouses make each other unhappy. But I've found that the most common Love Busters in marriage fall into just six categories: selfish demands, disrespectful judgments, angry outbursts, dishonesty, annoying habits, and independent behavior.

It's easy to justify all Love Busters. You may regard angry outbursts as a way to express your deepest emotions, disrespect as helping your spouse gain proper perspective, and a demand as simply encouraging your spouse to do what he or she should have done all along. Maybe you've convinced yourself that dishonesty protects your spouse, and that your annoying habits and independent behavior are just part of who you are.

But before you convince yourself there's nothing wrong with that behavior, think of the pain you inflict with these thoughtless acts. Whenever you cause your spouse's unhappiness, one thing's for sure—Love Bank withdrawals are taking place. So if you want to protect your love for each other, take some time to pinpoint which Love Busters have infected your marriage and then create a plan to throw them out.

Selfish Demands

When you request something you need, and the request is denied or ignored, what's your next instinct? Most of us move to a more forceful measure—we make a demand. But demands usually fail to get the job done, and they make us controlling and abusive.

> Demands and manipulation don't build cooperation, they build resentment.

Nobody likes to be told what to do. And if we could actually feel the effect our demands have on our spouse, we wouldn't make them. We certainly don't want our spouse making demands of us. But when we make a demand, we feel justified—a demand seems like a reasonable way to get what we need, including help with the responsibilities of raising children. But let me assure you: Demands won't get the help you need.

Without a doubt, you and your spouse need to motivate each other to help bear the burden of raising a family. But demands won't work. Your spouse will try to escape your abuse, and instead of helping you, he or she will avoid you as much as possible. Do you really

SOUND FAMILIAR?

As she walked through the living room, Lydia noticed what a mess everything was. The kids' toys were strewn all over the room, and a thick layer of dust covered everything. She asked her husband, who was watching TV, to straighten things up. But Nick didn't respond. "Clean this room right now!" Lydia shouted as she turned off the TV.

want to drive your spouse away, or do you want to encourage your spouse to help you?

Marriage isn't like the army; there are no sergeants and no privates. Neither you nor your spouse has a right to tell the other what to do. And when you try, you create a temporary solution at best. Your spouse may fulfill one demand, but what happens the next time the problem surfaces? Your spouse will give greater resistance, and your desires will become increasingly difficult to obtain. Demands and other forms of manipulation don't build cooperation; they build resentment.

So what's the alternative to selfish demands? It's thoughtful requests—getting what you need from each other by simply explaining what you'd like and asking your spouse how he or she would feel about fulfilling your request. If your spouse thinks the request will be unpleasant to fulfill, then instead of trying to force your spouse to do it, you discuss ways he or she could help you that wouldn't be unpleasant.

"I've already tried that, and it doesn't work," may be your immediate reaction. "What if my spouse just doesn't want to help?" That's where negotiation takes over. In the next chapter, you'll learn how to become a skilled negotiator who can accept a negative reaction and then find a way to create a positive reaction. But for now, I want you to be aware of the fact that demands will not solve your problem, and they make you controlling and abusive.

Disrespectful Judgments

Disrespectful judgments are usually cleverly disguised efforts to get what we

---

Try This

Next time you need something from your spouse, try writing your request down before you ask. Read it back to yourself as if you were the one on the receiving end. Are you asking how your spouse would feel about helping you? Are you giving your spouse the right to decline, or are you really making a demand that you expect your spouse to fulfill, regardless of how he or she may feel?

want. Instead of making an outright demand, we try to convince our spouse that his or her failure to do what we want is a personal shortcoming. We try to "straighten out" our spouse.

If our spouse doesn't spend much time with the kids, for example, we'll call him or her "lazy." All we really want is some help taking care of the children, but when our demands don't work, we turn to personal attacks. Without a doubt, demands are abusive, but disrespectful judgments can make demands seem merciful by comparison.

These attacks aren't necessarily intended to be mean-spirited. We often rationalize our disrespect by convincing ourselves that we're doing our spouse a favor. If they would only see the light of our superior opinions, we tell ourselves, they would be much happier. We're just pointing out their personal flaws to help them become better people.

But when we try to impose our opinions, we imply that they have poor judgment. And that's disrespectful. We may not say this in so

SOUND FAMILIAR?

Dave wanted to record every check written in their checkbook and keep a running total of their account balance. But Liz, his wife, would usually forget to make each entry, so they never really knew how much money was in their account at the end of the month. Dave had asked her to write down her purchases in the checkbook dozens of times, but she never really took the problem too seriously. She'd just call the bank and check her account balance every few days to make sure they weren't in the red.

One evening Dave decided to straighten Liz out. "Liz, you're not being very smart. Whenever you write a check and don't record it in the check register, you're asking for trouble. I want to help you learn to be a more responsible person, but you're sure making it difficult for me."

many words, but it's the clear message they hear. If we valued their judgment more, we would question our own opinions.

As I've mentioned, a disrespectful judgment is usually a sophisticated way to get what we want from our spouse. But even when we have pure motives, it's still a controlling and abusive strategy. It's controlling because it imposes our point of view on our spouse, and it's abusive because it causes our spouse to be unhappy. Disrespectful judgments are personally threatening, arrogant, and rude. And they make sizable withdrawals from the Love Bank.

> When we impose our opinions on our spouses, we imply that they have poor judgment.

When we're being disrespectful, we often fail to recognize it. We think we're being helpful when we're actually being hurtful. And all we feel is our own self-righteous belief that we're doing the right thing.

So how can you know if you're a perpetrator of disrespectful judgments? The simplest way to find out is to ask your spouse. You can't feel the effect of your disrespect, but he or she can. To help you ask the right questions, I've provided the following Disrespectful Judgments Questionnaire. Ask your spouse to complete this questionnaire now.

Disrespectful Judgments Questionnaire

Circle the number that best represents your feelings about the way your spouse tries to influence your attitudes, beliefs, and behavior. If you circle a number greater than 1 for any question, try to think of an example that you can share with your spouse and write it on a sheet of paper.

1. Do I ever try to "straighten you out"?

Almost Never			Sometimes			Much of the Time
1	2	3	4	5	6	7

2. Do I ever lecture you instead of respectfully discussing issues?

Almost Never			Sometimes			Much of the Time
1	2	3	4	5	6	7

3. Do I seem to feel that my opinion is superior to yours?

Almost Never			Sometimes		Much of the Time	
1	2	3	4	5	6	7

4. When we discuss an issue, do I interrupt you or talk so much that you are prevented from having a chance to explain your position?

Almost Never			Sometimes		Much of the Time	
1	2	3	4	5	6	7

5. Are you afraid to discuss your points of view with me?

Almost Never			Sometimes		Much of the Time	
1	2	3	4	5	6	7

6. Do I ever ridicule your point of view?

Almost Never			Sometimes		Much of the Time	
1	2	3	4	5	6	7

The scoring for this questionnaire is simple. Unless all of your spouse's answers are ones, you're probably engaging in disrespectful judgments. Almost all of us are guilty of this Love Buster from time to time, so don't be alarmed if you get some twos or threes. But if your spouse gives you any scores higher than four, your disrespectful judgments are rising to the level of abuse.

If your spouse identifies you as one who makes disrespectful judgments, you may be tempted to make yet another disrespectful judgment and claim that he or she is wrong! Resist that temptation at all costs, because in every case of abuse, the victim is a far better judge of its existence than the perpetrator. Take his or her word for it and start working on a plan to eliminate the disrespect.

I'm not saying that you shouldn't disagree with your spouse. But I want you to *respectfully* disagree. Present the information that brought you to your opinion. And then try to understand your spouse's reasoning, avoiding the temptation to ridicule it. Entertain the possibility that you might change your own mind instead of just pointing out how wrong your spouse is. That's how respectful persuasion works.

You see, each of you brings two things into your marriage—wisdom and foolishness. Your marriage will thrive when you blend your value systems, with each one's wisdom overriding the other's foolishness. By sharing your ideas and sorting through the pros and cons, you can create values superior to what either of you had alone. But unless you approach the task with mutual respect, the process won't work and you'll destroy your love for each other.

In the next chapter, I'll show you how to use respectful persuasion to help you make one of the most important decisions of your lives—how you'll raise your children. But if you use disrespectful judgments to try to impose your method of child training on each other, your conflicting goals and methods of discipline will leave your children rudderless, unsure of their values, and lacking respect for both of you.

On the other hand, if you use your combined wisdom to set valuable goals and create realistic methods of discipline, your children will feel secure and confident. They'll know that you have thought the issues through and have their best interests in mind.

> ### Try This
>
> Discover if disrespectful judgments have infected your marriage by completing the Disrespectful Judgments Questionnaire. Don't be defensive if your spouse considers some of your behavior to be disrespectful. Instead, start practicing respectful persuasion, which is described more fully in the next chapter.

Disrespectful judgments don't belong in your marriage. They don't solve problems—they only create resentment and destroy love. So if your marriage has been invaded by this Love Buster, try respectful persuasion.

Angry Outbursts

When demands don't produce results, and disrespect doesn't work either, people often resort to angry outbursts. In fact, demands, disrespect, and anger usually appear together—they define the typical fight. But all three of these strategies are abusive, controlling, and tragic. Instead of protecting each other from these destructive instincts, spouses unleash them to become the greatest source of each other's unhappiness.

Although anger is nothing more than an abusive way to get what we want or to punish someone for not giving us what we want, our instincts tell us it's a reasonable response to injustice. We feel that someone is deliberately making us unhappy (by not giving us what we want), and that it isn't fair. In our angry state, we're convinced that the offender will keep upsetting us until he or she is taught a lesson. Since we assume the person won't listen to reason, we try to punish him or her instead. That'll make 'em think twice about making us unhappy again!

Anger seems to offer a simple solution to our problem—just destroy the troublemaker. But if our spouse turns out to be the troublemaker, we hurt the one we've promised to cherish and protect. When we're angry, we don't care about our spouse's feelings, and we're willing to scorch the culprit if this prevents us from being hurt again. What a terrible way to treat our lover! And what a terrible example for our children!

In the end, we have nothing to gain from anger. Punishment doesn't solve marital problems—it makes them worse. When we become

SOUND FAMILIAR?

Tears were streaming down Pam's face as she watched Rick storm out of the room. They'd only been married for a year, and she knew he'd been under stress with the arrival of twin boys just ten months after the wedding. But she couldn't understand his latest tirade. Tonight he'd accused her of lying about her birth control so she could become pregnant. And he went on and on about how she was trying to drive them into bankruptcy with all of her spending.

angry with our spouse, we threaten his or her safety and security. So our spouse rises to the challenge and tries to destroy us in retaliation. Or our spouse becomes so afraid that he or she leaves us. When anger wins, love always loses.

Each of us has an arsenal of weapons we use when we're angry. If we think someone deserves to be punished, we unlock the gate and select an appropriate weapon. Sometimes the weapons are verbal (ridicule and sarcasm), sometimes they're devious plots to cause suffering, and sometimes they're physical. But they all have one thing in common: They're designed to hurt. And since our spouses are at such close range, we can use our weapons to hurt them the most.

> When anger wins, love always loses.

Some of the husbands and wives I've counseled have fairly harmless arsenals, maybe just a few awkward efforts at ridicule. Others are armed to thermonuclear proportions; their spouses' very lives are in danger. There's no excuse for an angry outburst, regardless of how benign your weapons are. But if your weapons are dangerous, and you have not learned to control your temper, you must find professional help in anger management. And I recommend that you and your spouse separate while you do so. Until you can guarantee your ability to control your temper, it's too dangerous for your spouse to be with you.

Domestic violence should not be tolerated. But the same can be said about lesser forms of angry outbursts. They not only destroy your love for each other, but they prevent you from solving any of your marital problems. If your spouse is afraid of your temper, he or she will avoid any discussion for fear that it could trigger your anger. It destroys all hope of finding a mutually agreeable solution.

As I will show you in the next chapter, the solution to marital problems is possible only when you can guarantee each other's safety when you negotiate. That means angry outbursts must be completely eliminated.

If you have difficulty controlling your angry outbursts and would like to overcome this Love Buster once and for all, you should begin with an awareness that it's something we do naturally—it's a habit that is developed by our instincts to get what we want. One of the most common excuses I hear is that angry outbursts feel so natural that they must be the right thing to do.

While we can't change our instincts, we can short-circuit their approach to a problem. If I have an instinct to have angry outbursts, it doesn't mean I am destined to go around losing my temper. I can create new habits that keep my anger in check. Habits that override inappropriate instincts are usually more difficult to create than habits that are not instinct driven, but it can be done. And in marriage, it must be done if you want to be in love with each other.

CONSIDER THIS

Never tolerate domestic abuse. Report every incident of physical abuse to the police. Even a slap across the face should be reported. When physical abuse is kept secret, it grows just like mold in a closet and becomes increasingly dangerous. But when it is made public to law enforcement, the perpetrator is forced to recognize the seriousness of the problem and do something about it. Some of the most successful outcomes I've witnessed in anger management have been with a spouse under the threat of jail time.

Children who must watch their parents engage in domestic violence are among the saddest children. Instead of seeing parents who love and care for each other, they see parents who are deliberately hurting each other. And then, when the fight is over, they watch their parents try to cover up the abuse and prevent anyone else from knowing what really happened. These children grow up to believe that domestic violence is justified under certain circumstances, and lying about it is also justified. They learn to be abusive and dishonest as adults.

If you struggle with angry outbursts, you should try to develop short-circuiting habits. Whenever you begin to feel angry, practice a behavior that can prevent an outburst. In the beginning, your new behavior will be a conscious choice, something you do regardless of how it feels. Walking away from a frustrating situation is one example of a short-circuiting behavior. Or you could try following a routine that relaxes your muscles and lowers adrenaline in your system. Eventually, with practice, the behavior that short-circuits your angry outbursts will become a habit. And whenever you begin to feel angry, the habit will kick in to overcome your angry outbursts.

Most anger management counselors recommend this short-circuiting technique alone. But I usually go one step further. I encourage clients to overcome all abusive behavior, beginning with selfish demands, because that's where abuse usually begins. From there, they eliminate disrespectful judgments, and then they're in a better position to get their angry outbursts under control.

You have no right to try to control your spouse, regardless of what he or she is doing. Once you accept this reality, you'll be more motivated to create habits that take the place of demands, disrespect, and anger.

Try This

If you or your spouse believes your angry outbursts are sometimes justified, you should seek professional help in anger management, because your mental and physical health is at risk. Angry outbursts are never justified, because they prevent you from finding the real solutions to marital problems and cause you to hurt the one you should protect.

If you use abusive and controlling strategies to get what you want, you'll set a horrible example for your children, and you'll probably lose your spouse's love. But if you learn how to resolve conflicts with thoughtful requests and respectful persuasion, you'll solve your problems and set a healthy example for your children. And you'll also protect your love for each other.

Dishonesty

If your spouse had an affair ten years ago that was a brief indiscretion, would you want to know about it?

If you had an affair ten years ago that you ended because you knew it was wrong, should you tell your spouse?

These are tough questions that go to the heart of our fourth Love Buster—dishonesty.

Dishonesty is the strangest of the six Love Busters. Obviously, no one likes dishonesty, but sometimes honesty seems even more damaging. What if the truth is more painful than a lie?

When a wife first learns her husband has been unfaithful, the pain is often so great that she wishes she had been left ignorant. When a husband discovers his wife's affair, it's like a knife in his heart—and he wonders if it would've been better not to have known. In fact, many marriage counselors advise clients to avoid telling spouses about past infidelity, saying that it's too painful for people to handle. Besides, if it's over and done with, why dredge up the sewage of the past?

It's this sort of confusion that leads some of the most well-intentioned husbands and wives to lie to each other, or at least give each other false impressions. They feel that dishonesty will help them protect each other's feelings.

SOUND FAMILIAR?

Stephanie quickly hid the toys in the basement closet. She'd promised her husband that she wouldn't buy more than three presents for their daughter Michelle's birthday. But she'd found two more toys she knew Michelle would love. *Oh well,* she thought to herself, *why does he have to be such a tightwad anyway? I'll just wrap two together so he won't know about the extra gifts until after Michelle opens them.*

But what kind of a relationship is that? The lie is a wall that comes between them. It's something hidden, a secret that can't be mentioned, yet it's right under the surface of every conversation. And dishonesty can be as addictive as a drug. One secret leads to another. So if you start using dishonesty to protect each other's feelings, where will it end?

That's why dishonesty is a strange Love Buster. Lies clearly hurt a relationship, but truth can also hurt, especially in the short term. It's no wonder that many couples continue in dishonesty—they feel they can't take the shock of facing the truth. But as a result, the marriage dies a slow death. Honesty, on the other hand, is like a flu shot. It may give you a short, sharp pain, but it keeps you healthier in the long run.

> Honesty is like a flu shot. It may give you a short, sharp pain, but it keeps you healthier in the long run.

In the case of infidelity, don't you think that your own affair would be one of the most important pieces of information about yourself? How could you ever expect to have an intimate relationship with someone to whom you cannot reveal your most inner feelings?

I'll admit that infidelity is an extreme example of something you would be tempted to lie about. But "little white lies" can be just as destructive when discovered, and there's even less justification for them. If it makes sense to be honest about something as hurtful as an affair, it makes even more sense to be honest about something more trivial, such as buying something that your spouse wouldn't have approved.

It's important to draw a distinction between the pain of a thoughtless act and the pain of knowing about a thoughtless act. Honesty sometimes creates pain—the pain of knowing that your spouse has been thoughtless. But it's really the thoughtless act itself that causes the deepest pain. Dishonesty may defer some of that pain, but it compounds the pain later and creates huge Love Bank withdrawals. The truth usually comes out eventually, and the months or years of hiding it not only creates an emotional barrier before it's revealed, but also destroys trust afterward.

Dishonesty also strangles compatibility. To create and sustain compatibility, you must lay your cards on the table. You must be honest about your thoughts, feelings, habits, likes, dislikes, personal history, daily activities, and plans for the future. When misinformation is part of the mix, you have little hope of making successful adjustments to each other. How can you find solutions to your problems if dishonesty makes you ignorant of the problem to begin with?

Honesty helps couples build compatibility and love because it tends to make our behavior more thoughtful. If we knew that everything we do and say would be televised and reviewed by all our friends, we'd be far less likely to engage in thoughtless acts. And honesty is like the television camera in our lives. If we're honest about what we do, we won't be as tempted to engage in thoughtless acts because we know those acts will always be revealed.

In an honest relationship, thoughtless acts are usually corrected. Bad habits are nipped in the bud. And couples can eliminate incompatible attitudes and behavior. But if these attitudes and behavior remain hidden, they are left to grow out of control.

> ### Try This
>
> Encourage your spouse to be honest with you by valuing honesty. Tell your spouse that you want honesty at all costs. And avoid punishing honesty with demands, disrespect, or anger when your spouse is honest with you.

If you or your spouse has a tendency to lie or distort the truth, chase that bad habit out of your marriage before it ruins everything.

Annoying Habits

When was the last time your spouse did something that annoyed you? Last week? Yesterday? An hour ago? Maybe your spouse is humming that irritating tune this very minute!

Annoying habits include personal mannerisms such as the way you eat, the way you clean up after yourself (or don't!), and the way you talk. And one of the frustrating things about annoying habits is that they don't seem all that important—but they still drive you crazy. It's not abuse or dishonesty, just annoyance. You should be able to shrug it off, but you can't. It's like the steady *drip-drip* of water torture. Annoying behavior will nickel and dime your Love Bank into bankruptcy.

When we're annoyed, we usually consider others inconsiderate, particularly when we've explained to them that their behavior bothers us and they continue to do it. It's not just the behavior itself, but the thought behind it—the idea that they just don't seem to care enough to stop it.

But when our behavior annoys others, we downplay the whole problem. It's just a little thing, we argue, so why make a federal case out of it? Why can't other people adjust?

As I've already mentioned, empathy is at the root of the problem. I often wish I could switch a couple's minds—Dan becomes Jane for a day and Jane becomes Dan. If they could only know what it felt like to experience their own insensitive behavior, they would be much more motivated to change.

But what can motivate you to change when you don't feel what your spouse feels? It begins with the realization that whenever you do something that bothers your spouse, you're making Love Bank withdrawals. Those annoying habits that don't seem so important are destroying your spouse's love for you. The complaints you hear are cries for help: *Please stop hurting me!* When you tell your spouse to stop complaining, you fail to understand the damage you are doing to your Love Bank account.

SOUND FAMILIAR?

Jill walked into the living room and noticed that there were magazines all over the floor again. She understood that her husband, Evan, liked to read while he was keeping his eye on their baby. But did he have to throw them on the floor when he was finished reading them?

If I've convinced you that your annoying habits can drain a Love Bank account, you may wonder where you should begin in trying to eliminate them. After all, there may be so many.

I suggest that you chip away at them systematically. Ask each other what it is that annoys you and write those habits down. Then put them in the order of how annoying they are, with the most annoying habits first. As you look at your lists, you may find that some habits can be easily eliminated—all it will take is a decision to end them, and they're a thing of the past. After eliminating these habits, those that remain will require a plan. So take on only three of the remaining habits at a time, from the top of the list down. After they are overcome, work on the next three. Eventually, every annoying habit on the list will be eliminated.

Try This

Create a list of each other's annoying habits, ranking which ones disturb you the most. Begin with the three most annoying habits from each list and get to work eliminating them.

Independent Behavior

Have you ever planned activities as if your spouse didn't exist? You didn't bother to ask how he or she felt but instead just went ahead and did what you pleased? If you have, you've invited the sixth Love Buster into your marriage—independent behavior.

This Love Buster represents all the activities you pursue that fail to take your spouse's feelings and interests into account. Whenever you do something that is good for you but bad for your spouse, it's an independent behavior. But when you marry, you are no longer independent—you are interdependent. Your spouse does exist, and he or she will feel the effects of almost everything you do. If you practice independent behavior, you'll create an incompatible lifestyle that will eventually destroy your love.

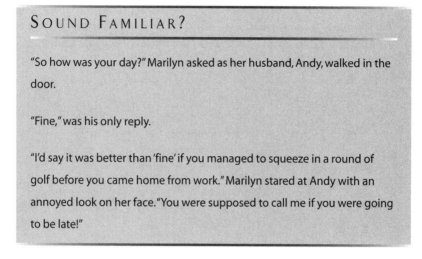

Since independent behavior is so tricky to identify and overcome, I've made it the topic of the next chapter. We'll look at this Love Buster more closely there, and I'll help you eliminate it from your marriage.

Busting Up the Love Busters

Wouldn't it be great if you and your spouse would never intentionally hurt each other again? Or if, when one of you hurt the other by mistake, you'd immediately apologize and take steps to avoid doing it again?

If you think about it, failure to avoid Love Busters can be a greater disaster in marriage than the failure to meet each other's intimate emotional needs. Once you unleash pain on your spouse, his or her desire to meet your intimate emotional needs evaporates. And your spouse will be in no mood to let you meet his or her needs. So Love Busters are double trouble: They make Love Bank withdrawals and prevent Love Bank deposits.

Be vigilant about defeating those sneaky Love Busters. They don't usually enter a relationship with a full-scale invasion. They often begin

> Love Busters are double
> trouble They make
> Love Bank withdrawals
> and prevent Love Bank
> deposits.

with a seemingly harmless foothold. But from this inauspicious beginning, they grow to become ugly, destructive habits that can ruin your marriage.

Are there Love Busters threatening your marriage? If they're just starting to creep in, you may have a hard time recognizing them for the monsters they are. But if you've struggled with Love Busters for a while, your Love Banks are probably running on empty.

Love Busters just don't belong in your marriage. They present a bad example for your children. And they'll eat away at your love for each other. So before the Love Busters destroy your love, start busting them up.

6

Declaration of Interdependence
The Policy of Joint Agreement

Tim and Frank had been working together in the banking indus-try for years. So when they decided to create a mortgage business of their own, they knew and respected each other's strengths. Tim tended to make conservative decisions, while Frank was a risk taker. Together, they made a great team—Frank pointing out good oppor-tunities and Tim wisely avoiding unhealthy deals. They discussed business matters frequently, seeking each other's advice before moving forward with new plans.

After fifteen years, their original office had grown into a network of branches spreading into several neighboring counties. Their friend-ship was as strong as ever, and they both enjoyed the financial benefits of a booming business.

That's when a new partner entered their team. Frank's son, Phil, had been working for their company for several years. Full of new ideas, he was eager to join the partnership team and make some changes. But after just one year as a partner, Phil had created huge problems for the business.

Ignoring the plans of the other partners, Phil often went ahead with his own schemes. When several of his ideas failed, the business began to suffer. And when Frank and Tim tried to rein Phil in, he resisted, and both clients and employees grew frustrated with the conflicting messages they received. Eventually Phil's dad, Frank, admitted that his own son would have to go. That painful decision set their business back on track again.

If you are the sole owner of a business, you have the right to make your own business decisions. But if you have a partner who owns an equal share of the business, you should consult with him or her and come to an agreement before making decisions. It just doesn't make sense for business partners to ignore each other. If they make decisions without joint agreement, like Phil did, their employees and clients become frustrated and confused, their business relationship deteriorates, and the business itself is bound to suffer.

> Marriage isn't a sole proprietorship—it's a partnership.

If that's true for business, it's particularly true for marriage. Marriage isn't a sole proprietorship—it's a partnership. When spouses ignore each other's interests and feelings, their marriage hits the rocks, and it's their children who end up most frustrated and confused.

But as a married couple, you're more than business partners—you're also lovers. And almost every decision you make will not only determine your success in raising a family, it will also affect your love for each other. Decisions that are made jointly are wise decisions that help build your love. But independent decisions are usually foolish decisions that destroy your love.

Dollars or Sense?

Already in early childhood, Tricia couldn't resist buying things she wanted. Her father tried to control her spending, but she would become so upset that he'd usually give in and hand her the money to buy what she wanted.

While Dan dated her, he'd buy her gifts just to see her reaction. She seemed to live for her next gift from him. Dan's generosity brought out the best in her, and within six months they were head over heels in love with each other.

As an executive in a growing company, Dan earned very good wages. But it never occurred to him that they were not enough to support Tricia's excessive buying habits.

In the first few years of marriage, he justified many of her acquisitions as necessities for their new home. But Tricia wasn't satisfied with her initial purchases—she'd be off buying replacement items before some of the originals were even delivered. And the closets in their home were soon so filled with clothes that she had to give many away to make room for new outfits.

When their first child, Jake, arrived, the problem only got worse. Dan and Tricia's financial pressures grew as they faced the added expenses of caring for Jake. And Tricia not only continued her own extravagant spending habits but also turned her shopping interests toward Jake's nursery, clothes, and toys. Before long, their baby had just about everything stores had to offer.

Dan became alarmed. "Tricia, I think it's time we discuss something. You're spending more than we can afford. I want you and Jake to have everything you need, but we must start watching our money more carefully."

Tricia was genuinely concerned. "Oh, Dan, are you having financial problems?" she asked.

"*We* are having financial problems! My income is better than ever, but I can't keep up with your spending," he complained. "We need to be on a budget. If I give you an allowance, will you stick to it?"

"Sure, I guess that's okay with me," she reluctantly agreed.

Dan worked out a budget for Tricia, but she didn't stick to it. When Dan brought up the subject, she shrugged it off as a bad month and promised to do better the next month. But she was already planning to redecorate the nursery—for the third time.

Dan decided to take matters into his own hands. "Tricia, I must put a stop to your irresponsible spending. I'm taking your name off

our checking account and credit cards. I'm sorry, but it's the only way
to solve the problem."

Tricia was terribly hurt. She knew she had a problem, but Dan was
treating her like a child. Even though he gave her a generous cash
allowance each week, she resented him for taking control of their
finances. So she opened her own credit card accounts and spent even
more money just to show him that he couldn't control her.

What should they do? How would you handle this problem? Tricia's
irresponsible spending is a good illustration of independent behavior.
It's a very common problem in marriage, but it's not usually quite
so extreme. Instead of a large income with even larger irresponsible
spending, most couples have the same problem on a much smaller
scale. One spouse tries to stick to a budget while the other feels justified in ignoring it. What should you do if your spouse, like Tricia,
is making independent decisions? And is there any good excuse for
you to be making them yourself?

A Subtle Love Buster

Most spouses have no problem seeing how selfish demands, disrespectful judgments, angry outbursts, dishonesty, and annoying
habits can wreck a marriage. But the damage caused by independent behavior—actions that don't take your spouse's feelings into
account—isn't so easy to see. And even when spouses know that
it's damaging their relationship, they often find it particularly
difficult to overcome this subtle Love Buster. So I've devoted
this chapter to helping you recognize and overcome independent
behavior.

At first glance, independent behavior in marriage might seem desirable and even essential. After all, who wants to give up their ability to
make independent choices when they marry? Wouldn't that cripple a
person—cause them to lose their very identity? And no one wants to
be clingy and dependent, or to have a spouse who's unable to make
any decisions of their own.

But independent behavior isn't the only alternative to unhealthy dependency. There's a far superior alternative that I call interdependency—spouses who behave in ways that take each other's feelings into account. And this alternative doesn't cause the slightest loss of identity.

Think about your own marriage for a moment. What could you do on your own that would have absolutely no effect on your spouse? It's probably a very short list. Almost everything you and your spouse do in marriage affects each other, from your decisions about personal hygiene to your decisions about child training.

> Independent behavior isn't the only alternative to unhealthy dependency. There's a far superior alternative— interdependency.

That means nearly everything you do makes either deposits or withdrawals from your spouse's Love Bank. So if you want to protect your love for each other, you must pay close attention to the way your behavior affects each other. Is your behavior making your spouse happy or unhappy?

Because independent behavior ignores your spouse's interests, it's likely to make him or her unhappy. Dependent behavior isn't the answer either, because it ignores your interests and will make you unhappy. But interdependent behavior takes the interests of both of you into account. It says, "I care about you, and I don't want to do anything that will hurt you. But I also care about how I feel." It enables you to stay in love with each other, because it leads to decisions that make both of you happy simultaneously. And it also creates the best environment for your children, where they learn to be thoughtful of others by watching you make thoughtful decisions.

The Policy of Joint Agreement

Independent behavior is so pervasive in marriage that I've made a rule that will help you learn to become interdependent. If you always follow this rule, every decision you and your spouse make will be inter-dependent. The Love Buster of independent behavior will become a thing of the past. I call this rule the **Policy of Joint Agreement:** *Never do anything without an enthusiastic agreement between you and your spouse.*

The Policy of Joint Agreement: Never do anything without an enthusiastic agreement between you and your spouse.

So what do you think? Does that sound crazy?

Interdependence goes against our instincts, so people often think this rule is insane. But the more you practice inter-dependence in your marriage, the more you'll recognize it as a breakthrough in making your marriage mutually fulfilling.

Interdependence gives your intelligence an opportunity to resolve conflicts instead of turning them over to your irrational emotions and instincts.

This rule probably brings two reactions to your mind. On the one hand, there's the part that requires your enthusiastic agreement before your spouse does anything. That doesn't sound so bad, does it? Wouldn't you like to know what your spouse is planning, so you can protect your own interests? But on the other hand, you may think it would be ridiculous to let your spouse's lack of enthusiasm prevent you from doing what you'd like to do. What if he or she says no to something you really want?

This takes us back to the problem of empathy. We all want our spouse to be thoughtful of *our* feelings, because we feel what our spouse does to us. But we tend to ignore our spouse's feelings, because we don't feel what we do to our spouse. If we were emotionally con-nected to each other so that we felt each other's pain, we'd behave very differently. We'd want to know how our behavior would affect each other—in advance—so we would avoid any pain to ourselves. And that's precisely what the Policy of Joint Agreement does. It gives us advance notice of how we will be affecting each other. While we can't actually feel the pain we inflict on each other, this agreement makes us behave as if we can.

Thoughtfulness at All Costs

The Policy of Joint Agreement helps you become sensitive to each other's feelings, especially when you don't feel like doing so. Since you're required to have each other's enthusiastic agreement before you do anything, it forces you to ask each other a very important question: "How do you feel about what I would like to do?"

That simple question helps you build empathy. You may not actually feel what your spouse feels, but at least you give your spouse the opportunity to tell you how he or she feels. And then, even when you find yourself in a thoughtless mood, the Policy of Joint Agreement forces you to be thoughtful.

You are now a team, not two independent individuals. You should work together to achieve objectives that benefit both of you simultaneously. Why should one of you consider your own interests so important that you can run roughshod over the interests of the other? That's a formula for marital disaster. And it presents a bad example for children.

When I first see a couple in marital crisis, they are usually living their lives as if the other hardly exists—making thoughtless decisions regularly because they don't care how the other feels. As a result, when I introduce the Policy of Joint Agreement, it seems irrational to them. They've created a way of life that is based on so many inconsiderate habits that the policy seems to threaten their very existence. At first, they don't want to abandon their thoughtless and insensitive behavior. But the more they try to follow the policy, the easier it becomes to reach agreement. They replace thoughtless habits with those that take each other's feelings into account. And they develop real compatibility—building a way of life that is comfortable for both of them.

No More Dictators

Unfortunately, most couples don't practice the Policy of Joint Agreement. Instead of using negotiation to reach mutual decisions, they usually handle conflict with the **Dictator Strategy.** This strategy assumes that one member of the family, usually the husband, has the right, wisdom, and compassion to make family decisions correctly. While other members of the family can lobby to have him (or her) take their interests into account, when he makes a decision, it's final.

Dictators haven't been known to be particularly wise or compassionate. They tend to make decisions in their own interest and at the expense of their citizens. And the same thing happens in marriage. When one spouse is given the right to make all final decisions, the other spouse usually suffers. Has this ever happened to you?

Those who have had unpleasant experiences with a dictator often modify their approach to problem solving by creating a second strategy, the **Dueling Dictators Strategy.** As resentment grows, the subordinate spouse decides to stage a coup, raising both spouses to dictator status.

Guess what happens when two dictators disagree? It's all-out war, with each side looking after their own interests. After the dust settles, the stronger and more determined spouse wins the decision, which means that his or her solution is put into effect. But the losing dictator is already plotting more carefully for the next battle.

Unfortunately, millions of unhappy couples use the Dueling Dictators Strategy. It makes problem solving unpleasant for all involved, but at least it seems fairer than the Dictator Strategy, because the spouses are alternately winners and losers. Instead of one spouse being victimized, *both* spouses are victimized!

Some couples resort to a third approach for marital conflict resolution, the **Anarchy Strategy.** This strategy gives up trying to resolve conflicts and takes the position of "every man for himself." A husband or wife, or sometimes both, just do whatever they want and refuse to do anything their spouse wants. When dictator strategies fail, couples grasp at anarchy as their last hope. But just like countries in anarchy, anarchic marriages become chaotic and soon fall apart.

There is another way for couples to handle conflict—a way that doesn't destroy their love for each other. It's the **Democracy Strategy,** by which husbands and wives don't make a decision until they're both in agreement. The Democracy Strategy for marital conflict requires unanimous consent. Neither spouse can impose their will on the other.

Unlike all the other strategies we've seen, the Democracy Strategy addresses conflicts and resolves them with no victims. The outcome of *every* decision is in the best interest of both spouses.

So why isn't the Democracy Strategy used in all or even most marriages?

> The *Democracy Strategy* helps couples handle conflict without destroying their love for each other.

Because we aren't born with an instinct for democracy. Instead, we're born with an instinct to get our way at any cost. That attitude puts the Dictator Strategy into play. And once that happens, the Dueling Dictator and Anarchy Strategies often are not far behind.

The Democracy Strategy doesn't seem as natural as the others—it requires time and thought. But it's the only sensible way to make marital decisions. It not only provides wise solutions to your problems, but it will also draw you much closer to each other emotionally.

The Policy of Joint Agreement makes the Democracy Strategy possible. It gives both spouses equal power and control over the choices to be made. *Never do anything without an enthusiastic agreement between you and your spouse.* That simple rule forces you to find a mutually acceptable solution before any action is taken. And how do you find that solution? Through the fine art of negotiation.

Negotiators, Take Your Places

When you receive an unenthusiastic response to the question "How do you feel about what I would like to do?" you have two choices:

Either abandon the idea or try to discover alternative ways of making it possible. That's where negotiation begins!

With practice, you and your spouse can become experts at getting what you need in ways that create mutual, enthusiastic agreement. Once you agree to this policy, fair negotiation will become a way of life for you. And you'll also be forced to avoid the controlling and abusive strategies of demands, disrespect, and anger. Since they can't possibly create enthusiastic agreement from your spouse, you'll replace them with thoughtful requests and respectful persuasion.

> With practice, you and your spouse can become experts at getting what you need from each other.

Does this all sound impossible to you? Maybe you're so used to making unilateral decisions that you've never developed the habit of considering your spouse's feelings. But trust me, if you practice following the Policy of Joint Agreement, you'll get used to asking, "How do you feel about what I would like to do?" The policy forces you to practice being considerate and to understand each other's concerns. And that will bring you a giant step forward in your ability to negotiate.

At first, asking the question "How would you feel?" will seem very strange to you, and even humorous. That's to be expected—because your instincts don't think in those terms. Yet that question is at the very core of every fair negotiation in life, and you must force yourselves to ask it until it becomes a habit.

But even after you've agreed to my rule, you may not be entirely familiar with what goes on between the question "How do you feel?" and the enthusiastic agreement. You may not have had much experience negotiating with each other.

So I suggest that you follow a step-by-step procedure that is used by almost all successful negotiators. Four simple guidelines will help you reach solutions that satisfy both of you and avoid dictators and anarchy. I call them the Four Guidelines for Successful Negotiation.

Guideline #1: Set ground rules to make negotiation pleasant
and safe.

Most couples view marital negotiation as a trip to the torture chamber. That's because their efforts are usually fruitless, and they come away from the experience battered and bruised. Who wants to negotiate when you have nothing but disappointment and pain to look forward to?

So before you begin to negotiate, set some basic ground rules to make sure you both enjoy the experience. Since you should negotiate as often as conflict arises, it should always be an enjoyable and safe experience for you both.

I suggest three basic ground rules.

Ground Rule #1: Try to be pleasant and cheerful throughout nego-tiations. It's fairly easy to start discussing an issue while in a good mood. But negotiations can open a can of worms and create negative emotional reactions. Your spouse may begin to feel uncomfortable about something you say. In fact, out of the clear blue, he or she may inform you that there will be no further discussion.

I know how upset and defensive couples can become when they first tell each other how they feel. So I tell them what I'm telling you—try to be as positive and cheerful as you can be, especially if your spouse says something that offends you.

Ground Rule #2: Put safety first—do not make demands, show disrespect, or become angry when you negotiate, even if your spouse does. Once the cat is out of the bag and you've told each other what is bothering you, you've entered one of the most dangerous phases of negotiation. If your feelings have been hurt, you will probably be tempted to retaliate. And unless you make a special effort to resist demands, disrespect, and anger, your negotiation will turn into an argument. But if you can keep each other safe, you'll be able to use your intelligence to help make the changes you both need.

Ground Rule #3: If you reach an impasse where you don't seem to be getting anywhere, or if one of you is starting to make demands, show disrespect, or become angry, stop negotiating and come back to the issue later. Just because you can't resolve a problem at a particular point in time doesn't mean you can't find an intelligent solution in the future. Don't let an impasse prevent you from giving yourself a chance to think about the issue. Let it incubate for a while, and you'll be amazed what your mind can do.

If your negotiation turns sour and one of you succumbs to the temptation of demands, disrespect, or anger, end the discussion by changing the subject to something more pleasant. After a brief pause, the offending spouse may apologize and wish to return to the subject that was so upsetting. But don't go back into the minefield until it has been swept clear of mines.

Guideline #2: Identify the problem from both perspectives.

Once you've set ground rules that guarantee a safe and enjoyable discussion, you're ready to negotiate. But where do you begin? First, you must state the problem and then try to understand it from the perspectives of both you and your spouse.

Most couples go into marital negotiation without doing their homework. They don't fully understand the problem itself, nor do they understand each other's perspectives. In many cases, they aren't even sure what they really want.

One of the responsibilities of a marriage counselor is to help couples clarify the issues that separate them. I'm amazed at how often the clarification itself solves the problem. "Oh, that's what we've been arguing about!" many couples say. And once they understand the issue and each other's opinions, they realize that the conflict is not as serious as they thought.

Respect is key to success in this phase of negotiation. Once the problem has been identified and you hear each other's perspectives, it's extremely important to understand each other instead of trying to straighten each other out. Remember that your goal is enthusiastic agreement, and that can't happen if you reject each other's perspectives. The only way you'll reach an enthusiastic agreement is to come up with a solution that accommodates both perspectives.

It's so much easier to negotiate the right way when your goal is enthusiastic agreement. It eliminates all the strategies that attempt to wear the other person down with abuse. But when I take demands, disrespect, and anger away from some couples, they are left feeling naked. They feel helpless about resolving an issue without these tools. They've rarely approached their problems with the goal of finding a win-win solution, and they simply don't know how to do it.

Is that how you and your spouse feel? If so, remember that with practice you'll begin to feel more comfortable approaching every conflict with the goal of mutual agreement. You'll learn to ask each other questions, not to embarrass each other but to gain a fuller understanding of what it would take to make each other happy. And when you think you have the information you need to consider win-win solutions, you're ready for the next step.

> **Try This**
>
> Before you start explaining each of your perspectives, take five minutes to write down your thoughts on paper. This will help clarify your concerns before you begin discussing the issue with your spouse, and it's a good way to avoid demands, disrespect, and anger.

Guideline #3: Brainstorm with abandon.

You've set the ground rules. You've identified the problem and discovered each other's perspective. Now you're ready for the creative part—looking for mutually enjoyable solutions. I know that can seem impossible if you and your spouse have drifted into incompatibility. But the climb back to compatibility has to start somewhere, and if you put your minds to it, you'll think of options that please you both.

When you brainstorm, quantity is often more important than quality. So let your minds run wild; go with any thought that might satisfy both of you. When you let your creative juices flow, you are more likely to find a lasting solution.

Resist the "I'll let you do what you want this time if you let me do what I want next time" solution. For example, if you want to go out with your friends after work, leaving your spouse with the children, you may suggest that you take the children another night so that your spouse can go out with his or her friends. But this isn't a win-win situation: One of you ends up unhappy whenever the other is happy. And once you've made this agreement, it can easily turn into a habit that pulls you apart.

Try This

Carry a pad of paper or a pocket notebook with you so you can write down possible solutions to a problem as you think of them throughout the day. Some problems may require days of thought and pages of ideas. Keep in mind your goal a solution that has mutual appeal.

Many well-intentioned but sadly misguided people recommend sacrifice in marriage. But it doesn't take much thought to realize that approach to marital problem solving is terribly flawed. After all, whoever does the sacrificing would suffer, and what caring couple wants that? They want mutual enjoyment with neither one suffering. It's only when we let our selfish instincts get the best of us that we expect our spouse to sacrifice for us.

You won't get very far if you allow yourself to think, *If she really loves me, she'll let me do this,* or *He'll do this for me if he cares about me.* Care in marriage should be mutual care, which means that both spouses want the other to be happy, and neither spouse wants the other to be unhappy. If you care about your spouse, you should never expect, or even accept, sacrifice as a solution to a problem.

Win-lose solutions are common in marriage because most couples don't understand how to arrive at win-win solutions. Their concept of fairness is that both spouses should suffer equally. But isn't it better to find solutions in which *neither* spouse suffers? With a little creativity, you can achieve this goal.

*Guideline #4: Choose the solution that meets the conditions
                of the Policy of Joint Agreement—mutual and
                enthusiastic agreement.*

After brainstorming, you'll have both good and bad solutions.
Good solutions are those both you and your spouse consider desirable.
Bad solutions, on the other hand, take the feelings of one spouse into
account at the expense of the other. The best solution is the one that
makes you and your spouse most enthusiastic.

Many problems are relatively easy to solve if you know you must
take each other's feelings into account. That's because you become
aware of what it will take to reach a mutual agreement. Instead of
considering options that are clearly not in your spouse's best interest, you think of options you know would make both you and your
spouse happy.

Consider the problem we mentioned above. You would like to
go out with your friends after work, leaving your spouse with the
children. Before you had agreed to the Policy of Joint Agreement,
you may have simply called your spouse to say you'd be late, or worse
yet, you may have arrived home late without having called. But now,
you must come to an enthusiastic agreement prior to the event. It
certainly restricts your freedom of choice, but on the other hand, it
protects your spouse from your thoughtless behavior.

After having presented your case, you'd probably hear immediate objections. Your spouse might not want you to be having fun
while he or she is home battling the kids. "Besides," your spouse
might mention, "our leisure activities should be with each other." In
response, you might suggest that your spouse drop the children off
with your parents (whom you will call to make the arrangements)
and join you.

If your spouse enthusiastically agrees, you are home free. Your
parents take your children for a couple of hours, and your spouse
joins you wherever it was you were planning to meet your friends.
Problem solved. In fact, if going out after work with friends becomes

Try This

It's much easier to have enthusiastic agreement regarding a short-term, experimental plan than a plan set in cement for life. If the plan doesn't work out for one spouse after you try it for a while, you can go back to brainstorming for a new one.

a regular event, you can plan ahead for it by arranging the child care in advance!

Of course, other problems can be more difficult to solve, involving many steps. But with some trial and error, you should eventually find a mutually agreeable solution.

If you find it almost impossible to come to an enthusiastic agreement regarding certain behavior, you may be struggling with an addiction. Whether it's drugs, alcohol, sex, gambling, or any other addictive behavior, you'll find that thoughtfulness is almost impossible to practice. The addiction is in complete control of your life, and you are helpless to protect your spouse from the suffering it causes. If that's the case, you must sweep the addiction out of your life with professional treatment before you can negotiate in the way I've suggested.

Does It Really Work?

If you follow the four guidelines I've suggested, negotiation can be an enjoyable way to learn about each other. And when you reach a solution that makes you both happy, you'll make substantial deposits into each other's Love Bank. In the end, the Policy of Joint Agreement not only helps you become great negotiators, it also protects your love for each other.

Remember Dan and Tricia, the couple I mentioned at the beginning of this chapter? When they came to my office for counseling, their marriage was in trouble. Tricia's irresponsible spending and Dan's dictatorial way of handling her problem were destroying their love for each other. If they didn't find a solution soon, their little son would grow up with divorced parents.

In my counseling office, I asked Tricia how she felt about budgets. "I hate them!" she shot back.

"Then why did you agree to go on a budget?"

"To get Dan off my back. He had no right telling me what to do, especially since I was just trying to be a good mother to our son. I knew at the time I wouldn't follow his little rules." She suddenly looked a bit guilty. "You won't tell Dan what I've just said, will you?"

> The Policy of Joint Agreement not only helps you become great negotiators, it also protects your love for each other.

Tricia's underlying motives had slipped out just long enough for me to get a glimpse of them, and they made everything crystal clear. When Dan had suggested they follow a budget, she had agreed just to get him to back off. She was not happy with the plan and felt that he had imposed it on her.

Dan hadn't really asked Tricia how she felt about the budget. He just drafted what he considered to be fair and asked her to follow it. But unless she became an enthusiastic partner in the final agreement, Dan could expect her to sabotage every plan he created.

I had to show Dan how to negotiate with Tricia instead of imposing his will on her. To reach an agreement that she would honor, he had to appeal to her interests. He was not accustomed to this approach, nor was she used to expressing her feelings openly. But I encouraged them to adopt the Policy of Joint Agreement. That meant their budget had to fit Tricia's view of fairness. And once the budget was created, she could not make purchases outside the budget unless it was with Dan's enthusiastic agreement.

Tricia knew that she had been failing to take Dan's feelings into account. And Dan knew that his solution to her problem spending had failed to take her feelings into account. By finding a solution that took the feelings of *both* into account, their marriage would thrive. And they had to begin with an agreement not to do anything until they found that solution.

Tricia and Dan spent an entire weekend hammering out a budget they could agree to enthusiastically. An item was even added that allowed her to be an impulsive spender once in a while—as long as it was within limits. With that agreement, her credit cards and checkbook were returned to her, and she promised to follow the Policy of Joint Agreement—not to spend any money outside the budget unless Dan agreed in advance.

Try This

To avoid arguments about money, use the Policy of Joint Agreement to create a budget. And then spend outside the budget only if you are both in enthusiastic agreement. Review your budget three months later to be sure you are still in agreement about each item.

But within three days she'd already broken her promise. She had gone shopping, found an outfit she liked that was priced far above her budget, and bought it without discussing her decision with Dan. He was furious when he discovered it.

She had agreed to the Policy of Joint Agreement and was enthusiastic about their new budget. But when it came to shopping, she couldn't follow it. Remember what I mentioned earlier—if you can't follow the policy after you've agreed to it, it's likely that you have an addiction. It turned out that Tricia was addicted to shopping. She couldn't resist buying something whenever she was in a shopping center. I suspected this was the case from the beginning, but Tricia needed to see it for herself so she could be part of the solution.

Now negotiation could begin regarding her addiction.

At first, whenever they started to discuss the issue of Tricia's spending, Dan would make demands and Tricia would respond with an angry outburst. So they usually avoided discussion entirely. But Dan learned to make the discussion more pleasant for both of them by not making demands or showing disrespect toward Tricia. And Tricia learned to control her temper, which was even easier when Dan treated her respectfully.

They moved on to the second step, identifying the problem with mutual respect from both of their perspectives. Tricia's rationale for compulsive buying was not even convincing to her, and yet Dan said nothing disparaging when she explained her motives. After hearing about her desire to dress well and give their son the best, Dan simply explained that he wanted the same things. But he told her how deeply offended he felt when she broke her promises to curb her spending. And he explained that her shopping could eventually drive them to financial ruin—an outcome he wanted to avoid for their sakes and for the sake of their son.

By the end of their conversation, Tricia was in tears. She admitted that she had a serious spending problem and that she wanted to solve it in a way that required a radical approach. She actually suggested the same plan Dan had originally tried to force on her. But this time it was also her plan. She decided that the best way for her to control her spending was to get rid of credit cards and their checking account. And she shopped with the cash that they both agreed they could afford.

You see, it wasn't that Dan's plan was so bad. But it was *his* plan, not *their* plan. Once they started to bargain with each other using enthusiastic agreement as their goal, she felt in control of the process and the outcome. And eventually she came to the same conclusion as Dan did—enthusiastically!

Practice Makes Perfect

As you've been reading my guidelines for successful negotiation, you may have been wondering if you have what it takes to build a lifetime of love. It may just seem like too much to remember.

But thankfully, once you establish the habit of negotiating with each other, it will be easy to run through the steps whenever there is a problem to solve. Whatever it is you want can be attained on autopilot. And that's particularly true when it comes to maintaining a romantic relationship. If you're in the habit of meeting intimate

emotional needs for each other and are in the habit of avoiding Love
Busters like independent behavior, your romantic relationship can
hum right along without much effort on
your part.

> Once you establish the
> habit of negotiating with
> each other, whatever
> it is you want can be
> attained on autopilot.

If you and your spouse have found
yourselves acting more like dictators than
sweethearts, you are not in the habit of
negotiating. But you can get into that
habit by practicing the guidelines I've
suggested. Any behavior can become
automatic and almost effortless when re-
peated often enough. So I suggest the following exercise to build the
habits of successful negotiation.

Go to a grocery store together, without your children, and for
about thirty minutes select items for your cart that you both would
be enthusiastic about buying. This should be "imaginary" buying,
and you don't need to actually purchase any of the items in your cart
when you're finished. I chose this exercise so you will have a chance
to make decisions on an issue that has no real practical consequences
for either of you. That way, you can avoid the emotional reactions
that accompany real conflicts you may be having.

If one of you wants an item that the other cannot be enthusiastic
about buying, negotiate with that spouse and try to create enthusiasm. But avoid making bargains that let you have one item that your
spouse doesn't like in exchange for your spouse having an item you
don't like. Make sure that every item is chosen with an enthusiastic
agreement. The very act of asking each other how you feel regarding
each item in question, and holding off on making a decision until
you have agreement, is an extremely important habit to learn if you
want to become compatible.

Repeat this exercise on several occasions until you can fill your
cart with groceries in the thirty minutes you have scheduled. Each
time you begin, you can go right to the items you've already agreed
to purchase, put them in your cart, and negotiate about new items.
When the cart is eventually filled, it will symbolize a total lifestyle

in which every aspect of your life is for your mutual benefit. It's a lifestyle you both can enjoy.

When you think you've gotten the hang of coming to an enthusiastic agreement about groceries, tackle some real conflicts you've been unable to resolve. You'll probably be amazed at how quickly the Policy of Joint Agreement takes root. And you'll see your marriage move from mediocre to amazing.

A UNITED
APPROACH
TO PARENTING

Ready for Kids?

Deciding to Expand Your Family

"First comes love, then comes marriage, then comes Susie in a baby carriage." Is that really the way it goes? Not necessarily. In these days of effective birth control, couples have other choices. They can postpone children or decide not to have them at all. And they can control when and how many children they add to their family after the firstborn arrives. But these decisions often can be extremely difficult to make, especially if spouses are not skilled in negotiating with each other.

Jessica wanted children, and she wanted them right after she was married. While dating Brent, she knew he didn't like children that well, but she specifically asked him if he was willing to have them and he said yes. From her perspective, it was a commitment. She wouldn't have married him if children were not in their future together. But after marriage, he told her that he didn't think he could deal with children in his life. He told her that he could change his mind, but he needed time to think about it.

"What am I supposed to do?" Jessica asked me in desperation. "How much time does he need to think about this? I love him a lot, but I also want to fulfill my dream of having children. I'm so confused, and thoughts of this whole situation are just making me sick!"

Building a Lifestyle Together

The best marriages are a blending of two people—two becoming one. While each person maintains his and her unique personality and interests, they both deliberately integrate those interests to form a relationship that is not only romantic but also mutually advantageous. When it's done right, each person becomes a happier and better person.

Creating a new way of life together is like building a brick home in which each brick represents a lifestyle decision. And those decisions are some of the most important decisions of life—where you'll live, how you'll spend money, what your traditions will be, and everything else that creates your new way of life. If a decision is mutually beneficial, the brick is strong. But if a decision benefits one spouse at the expense of the other, the brick will crumble under pressure.

> Creating a lifestyle together is like building a brick home—if decisions are mutually beneficial, the bricks are strong. But if a decision benefits one spouse at the expense of the other, the bricks will crumble under pressure.

A lifestyle made up of weak bricks will be very disappointing. You'll not have what you really want in life. And your romantic relationship will suffer because one of you will be unhappy much of the time. Only a lifestyle made up of strong bricks will make your marriage successful, and only the Policy of Joint Agreement guarantees strong bricks.

I've already touched on two of these important lifestyle decisions—finances and careers. If you get into the habit of using the

Policy of Undivided Attention and Policy of Joint Agreement to make financial and career decisions, you'll avoid many of the common mistakes made by couples later in life. You'll create an entire lifestyle made of strong bricks.

But there's one other lifestyle choice that's even more important than your career or how you spend and earn money—it's if and when you will add children to your family. Whether it's having a first child or a fifth, I encourage you to make that decision with the same thoughtfulness that you make all of your decisions. And in this chapter, I'll show you how to do it.

When Spouses Don't See Eye to Eye

In my seminars, I often rhetorically ask the audience if they discussed preconditions for their marriages. For example, did anyone ask the other, "Will you agree to be gainfully employed throughout our marriage?" After all, some people have so much trouble finding a suitable career that they spend their lifetimes chronically unemployed.

Another question might be, "Will you agree to have sex with me regularly after marriage?" What if a spouse at some point during marriage refuses to make love for, say, three years (not an uncommon experience). Should willingness to have sex be a precondition for marriage?

"Will you agree to show affection to me?"

"Will you agree to take time out of your busy schedule to give me your undivided attention?"

"Will you agree to be honest with me?"

"Will you agree not to hit me?"

"Will you agree not to have an affair?"

I could go on and on with conditions that most of us assume will be met when we marry. But these preconditions are rarely stated, except the last one about having an affair. In most wedding vows, we usually do promise to be faithful.

There are reasons people tend not to state preconditions for marriage. Marriage itself is usually considered to be more important than marital expectations. And so when you marry, you agree to share your life with another person "for better or for worse," even if your expectations aren't realized. That's why specific expectations, such as having sex, being affectionate, earning a living, or even having children, are not usually stated in the vows.

When Jessica asked Brent before marriage if he wanted children, he didn't think she was presenting one of her preconditions for marriage. He thought she was just curious to know how he felt at that point in time, and so he said yes. It didn't occur to him that they would not have married if his answer had been no.

While it's true that we usually set few preconditions for marriage, the realization of our expectations is extremely important in determining a marriage's success. Unless you meet each other's expectations regarding sex, affection, employment, and other needs, your marriage isn't likely to be very fulfilling. And if you fail to meet expectations for protection, such as avoiding physical violence and infidelity, your marriage won't last very long.

But what about having children? Is this an expectation that should also be met? The need to have and raise children is not one of the four intimate emotional needs I emphasize in this book, but I've found it to be so important, especially for women, that I have included it among the ten most important emotional needs in marriage (see Appendix A). I call it the need for **family commitment,** and I'll describe it more fully in later chapters.

But for now, I want you to recognize this need as a very important expectation. In fact, it's so important that most women, like Jessica, can't imagine a marriage without its fulfillment. For them, it's an important precondition for marriage. While it's reasonable to consider willingness to have children as a precondition for marriage, many couples don't discuss it until they are married. And then they sometimes discover they have very different perspectives. What should be done then?

There are also couples like Jessica and Brent who thought they were in agreement prior to marriage, but then one spouse changes his or her mind after marriage. How should that conflict be resolved?

These and similar problems are very difficult to resolve, yet they're common in marriage. If you are facing any of these issues, I think you'll find this chapter to be helpful. But if you've agreed to the children you have, and neither of you has any desire to add to your family, skip this chapter and go directly to chapter 8, "Rules of the House."

When Your Spouse Says No

All emotional needs are best met with enthusiasm, and the need for family commitment is no exception. If a husband reluctantly agrees to have children and then reluctantly assumes his responsibility to raise them, his wife is likely to experience frustration. So saying yes to having children is not enough.

Consider affection—how satisfying would it be if your spouse were to hug you reluctantly? What about sexual fulfillment, or intimate conversation, or recreational companionship? When you stop to think of it, these emotional needs are met best when the one meeting the need enjoys the experience.

The need for family commitment is especially sensitive to mutual enthusiasm and enjoyment. Even if your spouse were to sign a legal document that commits him or her to raising children, it wouldn't mean much unless he or she were enthusiastic about the decision.

If your spouse doesn't want to have children right now, I give you the same advice that I gave Jessica. For your sake, for the sake of your unborn children, and for the sake of your spouse, wait to have children until

> For the sake of your unborn children, your spouse, and yourself, wait to have children until you have your spouse's enthusiastic agreement.

you have your spouse's enthusiastic agreement. Having children, like any other objective in marriage, makes sense only when you and your spouse share enthusiasm for the objective and want to carry it out together.

But enthusiastic agreement doesn't come easily. It usually requires some negotiating. And this is especially true when it comes to making important decisions such as starting or adding to your family.

Jessica could have obtained her husband's reluctant agreement to have children. If she reminded him how he had indicated a willingness to have children before they married, and how her clock was ticking, he probably would have given in. But a reluctant agreement wouldn't have made her happy, and the arrival of their child might have ended their marriage.

The difference between a reluctant agreement and an enthusiastic agreement is usually depth of understanding. The more you understand each other, the easier it is to discover the conditions that will make you enthusiastic about a decision. Reluctance simply means that there are obstacles to remove, and once they are gone, the coast is clear.

That's what respectful persuasion is all about—removing obstacles. There are good reasons why some husbands, and some wives for that matter, are reluctant to have children. So as you address those concerns and create ways of resolving the problems they expose, you can eventually find yourselves in complete agreement.

> There are good reasons why some husbands and wives are reluctant to have children.

But before I mention some of the most common concerns regarding children, let me remind you again how to negotiate successfully in marriage. Since desires about having children can be a very emotional topic, it's especially important for you to follow the Four Guidelines to Successful Negotiation. Here's how you would use them to resolve this important conflict:

1. **Set ground rules to make negotiations pleasant and safe.** Before you start to discuss having children with your spouse, agree with each other that you both will follow these rules. First, be pleasant and cheerful throughout your discussion of the issue. Second, put safety first—don't threaten to cause pain or suffering when you negotiate, even if your spouse does so. And finally, if you reach an impasse, stop for a while and come back to the issue later. Your negotiations should accept and respect your differences of opinion.

2. **Identify the advantages and disadvantages of having children from the perspectives of both you and your spouse.** Explain why you would like to have a child—how it would meet one of your most important emotional needs. Then listen respectfully to any objections your spouse might have. Don't interrupt each other or lecture each other on the subject, and try to understand the pros and cons that each of you bring into the discussion. Be sure you don't argue with each other—just get to know the facts about how each of you feels so you know what the obstacles are and how you can try to remove them.

3. **Brainstorm solutions with abandon.** Take some time thinking up ways to resolve the conflict, and don't correct each other when you hear of a plan you don't like—you'll have a chance to do that later. Your spouse may suggest that you get a puppy instead of a child or that you can have as many children as you want as long as you don't expect his help. Don't say anything—just write it down along with other suggestions. If you give your intelligence a chance to flex its muscle, you'll have a long list of possible solutions.

4. **Choose the solution that is appealing to both of you.** Scattered within your list you'll likely find a solution that both of you would find attractive. In fact, the more you discuss the issue of parenthood, the more likely it is that you will create the conditions that will make you better parents and better lovers.

Overcoming Common Objections

Most couples are not like Jessica and Brent. They have little trouble deciding to raise a family, and they usually make the decision with enthusiasm. But there are an increasing number of spouses, especially those with divorced parents, who express reluctance. If your spouse isn't sure that he or she wants to raise children, you are likely to hear the following objections.

Children have always annoyed me—I wouldn't be a good parent.

This is how Jessica's husband felt. He thought he would not be a good father because he couldn't imagine spending most of his leisure time baby-sitting. Quite frankly, this also worried my wife, Joyce. She found children very irritating and as a result did very little baby-sitting as a teenager. But as soon as she had children of her own, she loved being a mother. The change in her attitude had something to do with the fact that they were her own children. But it also had something to do with the way she raised our children—we used a lot of baby-sitters when our children were young.

And that's what Jessica and Brent needed to think about before their children arrived—how much and what kind of attention would he be expected to give them?

> Baby-sit other people's children and discover how you could comfortably share responsibilities for your own children.

When couples have a serious conflict, I usually suggest they test some solutions before actually implementing any of them. This allows them to consider worthy alternatives even though one spouse may not yet be enthusiastic about it. While that approach can work for meeting most emotional needs, in the case of having children, how can you test a solution without actually having a child?

One possibility is to baby-sit other people's children. While it's true that they are not your children and your spouse may react to baby-sitting the way my wife, Joyce, reacted, there are important lessons you could learn. By watching your friends' children while they go out, you can discover how you would comfortably share the responsibility for your own children.

How would you divide tasks so that neither of you felt suffocated? How would you preserve your privacy so that you could continue to meet each other's intimate emotional needs the same way you meet them now? How would you avoid trying to escape it all by forming new friendships and activities that don't include your spouse or the children?

Your first baby-sitting experience may turn into a disaster because you've never considered some of these questions. In fact, it may be so bad that it decreases your willingness to have children. But as you begin to make wise baby-sitting decisions that take each other's feelings into account, you may become so comfortable with it that you will be the envy of all your friends—a couple who loves children so much that they would rather baby-sit than spend a night out! By then you'll be ready to care for your own.

When we have a child, I'll gain a mother but lose a lover.

Most husbands don't see this problem coming until it's too late. But if your husband saw the loss of the romantic relationship as soon as children arrived in his friends' marriages, he has a point that shouldn't be ignored.

One of your objectives in life may be to raise children. But you married because you were in love, and the quality of your marriage depends on your ability to sustain that love. There are many who forget this basic fact, and as soon as a child arrives, their care for each other drops more than just a peg. I've had scores of men complain to me that their wives have told them, "We must

> Some new parents say, "We must now care for our children more than we care for each other." That, of course, is the announcement of marital disaster on the horizon.

now care for our children more than we care for each other." That, of
course, is the announcement of marital disaster on the horizon.

And it isn't just wives who can turn off romance after the arrival of
children. Husbands too can be so overwhelmed with the responsibility
that they pour themselves into their careers as a way of earning more
money to feed the family. No time is left to meet intimate emotional
needs, and as a result, the romantic relationship that bound them
together in marriage ends.

I've already dealt with how to maintain a romantic relationship
after children arrive, and I'll continue to discuss the issue throughout
this book, so I won't say anything more about it here. But if you take
my advice, you won't lose each other as lovers when your children
arrive.

If we divorce, I'll be paying child support for the rest of my life.

For many men, children conjure up visions of burdensome child
support, awkward visitation, and endless legal expenses. If you're having any trouble getting along now, once a child comes along, your
marriage will probably get worse. It may even end, and your husband
may be thinking about what that entails.

If his objection is a fear of divorce, it's certainly worth removing,
whether or not you have children.

Find solutions to unresolved conflicts in your marriage—needs that
are not being met, Love Busters that are hurting you, and thoughtless
decisions that are pulling you apart. And don't have any more children
until these problems are solved. Children can make a great marriage
even greater, but they tend to make a failing marriage much worse.

If your spouse is afraid of divorce, this fear is certainly worth removing, whether or not you have children.

There are three legs to the romantic love stool, and all three are essential to its health. The first leg is to deposit the most love units by following the Policy of Undivided Attention to meet each other's intimate emotional needs. The second leg is to avoid withdrawing love units by overcoming habits that cause each other to be unhappy—Love Busters. And the third leg is using the Policy of Joint Agreement to create a lifestyle that benefits both of you.

If one leg of the romantic love stool is missing, the stool will not support your relationship. Love Bank deposits will not be made and withdrawals will drain your accounts. And if you bring children onto this scene, you'll probably make matters worse. So if your romantic relationship needs some repair, you should postpone having children until it's fixed.

Now is a great time to set these three legs securely into position. By addressing these important issues, you can create habits that will make having a great marriage seem almost effortless later on, when life becomes much more complicated. And once all three are in place, you'll be ready to raise happy and successful children.

When the Final Answer Is No

After discussing each other's perspectives on having children and understanding the obstacles, it's possible that adding children to your family is simply not in the best interest of your spouse—he or she may never agree to it with enthusiasm. If that's the case, my advice would be not to have more children.

The quality of a marriage relationship should be a couple's highest priority. Once that's achieved, they can mutually agree to their objectives in a most remarkable way. But even when a marriage relationship is good, it's foolish to have children if they are not in the best interest of one spouse.

> The quality of a marriage relationship should be a couple's highest priority.

But what if you feel resentful over this decision? How can you overcome that feeling?

There are two kinds of resentment in marriage: (1) Resentment from having been forced by your spouse to do something you didn't want to do, and (2) resentment from having been prevented by your spouse from doing what you wanted to do.

I regard the first kind of resentment as far worse than the second. This is why: Whenever you're prevented from doing something, there's always the option to do something else that would be of equal value to you. And it could also be something that would have your spouse's enthusiastic agreement.

But when you're forced to abide by your spouse's agenda and made to do something you don't like, there are no choices—you're trapped. Remember, just because you don't have children does not mean you can't have something else in your life that is also fulfilling. And if your spouse is simply refusing to add more children to your current family, you still have the opportunity to be a great parent to those you already have.

Fairness is a common issue in marriage, and the Policy of Joint Agreement gets to the heart of that issue. Fair turns out to be whatever is in the best interest of both you and your spouse. It's that simple. The Policy of Joint Agreement prevents you from trying to create a lifestyle in which one of you suffers so the other can flourish. So unless you both flourish simultaneously, you should continue to negotiate until you find a compatible lifestyle.

In the case of having children, fairness can be hard to swallow when it means you can't add to, or even start, a family. But it would be even harder for your children to deal with parents who have a broken marriage because one of them forced children onto the other. Instead of harboring resentment over the issue, try to discover other objectives that could bring fulfillment to both of you.

Planning Ahead

So do you think you're ready to have more children? If you and your spouse have discussed the answer to that question and have come to an agreement by using the negotiating skills we talked about earlier in the chapter, I recommend that you also discuss specifics regarding how you'll raise the kids and divide responsibilities. Your plan should include a guarantee that your romantic relationship won't suffer with the arrival of children.

You should create a solid child-training plan. This topic, child-training goals and methods, is one of the most important you'll ever discuss with each other. But sadly, most parents don't really give it much thought until their children arrive. And many don't even discuss it then. Hundreds of couples I've counseled have waited until their teenage children were in serious trouble before discussing this crucial issue with each other. Don't make this mistake! There's no time like the present to come to grips with a child-training plan.

You should also decide how you will divide domestic responsibilities. And one thing's for sure—there will be more of them when you add children to your family.

In the next two chapters, I'll help you through the issues of child training. You'll learn how to choose a child-training plan that will make your children happy and successful as adults. And then in chapter 10, you'll learn how to divide domestic responsibilities fairly—so that neither of you is exhausted yet the job gets done.

But none of these plans will be at the expense of your romantic relationship. In fact, they will help make your marriage even more fulfilling than it is now. And the next time someone asks you, "Are you ready for kids?" you'll be able to answer in the affirmative—enthusiastically!

8

Rules of the House

Deciding on Child-Training Goals and Methods

L isa had plenty of opportunities to observe children—she was a salesclerk in the toy section of a department store. One day, as she was helping a woman with her purchases, the woman's son walked to a nearby display of stuffed animals and returned with a stuffed giraffe in his arms. "Mom, can we get it?" he asked with hopeful eyes.

His mom quietly responded, "I'm sorry, Ethan, but you know that we're here to buy a birthday gift for your sister, not new toys for you. Now put it back." Ethan's little shoulders slumped, but he walked to the shelves and slowly put the giraffe in place.

Lisa was impressed with Ethan's obedience, and she congratulated the young mother for raising such a well-behaved little boy. Just the day before, she'd watched a little girl throw a huge tantrum because she couldn't have a toy she wanted. And the girl's mom made matters worse by throwing a fit herself. She actually stormed out of the store without her daughter, yelling at her as she was leaving. But her abandoned daughter had the last word. "I hate you! And I hope you never come back!"

As Lisa tried to console the daughter, she thought to herself, *Wow, that mother has really messed up this poor little girl.*

Is There a Secret to Parenting Success?

Should Ethan's mother get credit for his good behavior? And should the mothers of children who misbehave be blamed? As someone who's spent his professional career counseling families, I'm convinced that parents should get much of the credit—and blame—for how their children turn out. That's because I've witnessed so many success stories of parents who have turned their children around by changing their child-training goals and methods.

> I'm convinced that parents should get much of the credit—and blame—for how their children turn out.

I've seen children like the abandoned girl become as well mannered as Ethan. But, more importantly, I've also seen these obedient children grow up to become happy and successful adults. Without a change in their parents' approach to child training, though, there might have been a tragic outcome.

Granted, some parents have an easier time raising their children than others. I'm sure genetics is one factor. Some parents seem to be born to do the right thing—or the wrong thing. Their instincts can help them or hurt them when it comes to knowing how to train children. Family background is another factor. Having wise parents is certainly an advantage when it comes to having children yourself.

But instincts and background are not the only factors that determine how children are raised. There's also education and training. You can learn how to raise successful children in spite of your flawed instincts or background. You can learn how to provide your children with tools that will serve them well throughout life, even if it doesn't come naturally or even if you were not given those tools yourself as you were growing up. And that's what parenting is all about—preparing children for life.

My counseling emphasizes modeling as a training method. I tell parents that they teach their children how to behave by their own example. Granted, children must be told what to do, but actions really do speak louder than words. So if parents expect their children to be thoughtful, they must demonstrate it in the way they treat each other. And they do this best by following the Policy of Joint Agreement.

> When it comes to child training, actions really do speak louder than words.

I also emphasize the importance of being in love as an essential part of parenting. By doing what it takes to insure your love for each other, you make a most important contribution to the happiness and success of your children. So I use the Policy of Undivided Attention to help parents carve out time to meet each other's intimate emotional needs.

To help illustrate how I teach these goals to parents, join me in a series of counseling sessions with Beth and Craig, a couple who came to me for advice on parenting. In the five three-hour sessions we had together, they learned some important lessons about child training. But they also discovered how the quality of their marriage would affect the success of their children. You may not have experienced their specific situation, but if you're looking for ways to be great parents and great lovers, this case study will point you in the right direction.

Genes and Baggage

Beth and Craig's counseling with me was a first wedding anniversary gift from Beth's mom, Ann, who was worried about her daughter's future as a wife and mother. They were expecting their first child within a few months, and Ann thought they should be educated in child training.

Ann had good reason to want her daughter and son-in-law to have advance education—they both came from broken homes, and Ann had been an abusive mother. Her angry outbursts were eventually brought under control, but not before Beth's injuries had been noticed at school and reported to Child Protection Services. That's how I had come to know Ann and Beth—I was the counselor Ann was required to see for anger management training.

Beth had two strikes against her. Her mother, who was divorced when Beth was only four, physically abused her throughout most of her early childhood. And Beth had been born with the same emotional predisposition to angry outbursts as her mom. Could she overcome the genetic predispositions that she'd inherited? And could a few counseling sessions compensate for her tragic background?

Before Beth and Craig had their first appointment with me, I asked them to write down some child-training goals. Neither of them had excelled in writing term papers, so my assignment was met with a less than enthusiastic response. But they managed to write down a few thoughts on the subject, and it encouraged them to start thinking about their goals. That's all I really wanted.

Session 1 Child-Training Goals

I'll have to admit that when Joyce and I were first married, we didn't give much thought to what our children should learn. And Beth and Craig's homework reports reflected the same poor preparation. He wanted his children to stay out of trouble, and she made a few references to honesty and ambition. But they both admitted they weren't sure what they wanted for their children.

> Many parents haven't given much thought to what they want their children to learn.

So in our first session together, we discussed training objectives that they both could enthusiastically support. As they tried to describe goals that made sense to them, they ran into conflict almost immediately.

Having been raised by divorced parents, they both had learned to value their independence. They'd had to take care of themselves in an environment in which loving parents were not there to protect them. Unlike Beth, Craig had not suffered physical abuse by either of his parents, but he had experienced more than his share of neglect. So he wanted his children to learn how to survive in a world of uncaring people.

"My kids should learn that there's only one person you can really trust—yourself," Craig announced. He wanted them to learn not to depend on anyone for help—to be as independent as he thought he had become.

Beth could understand his reasoning, but there was something about it that didn't seem right to her.

"Craig, if we're loving parents, why should our children feel that no one really cares about them?" she asked. In spite of the fact that she had not been given the care she'd needed, she was hoping her children would trust her to care for them.

"Nothing is certain in life, especially when it comes to people caring for you," he replied. "The sooner they learn that fact, the better off they'll be when they're on their own."

Beth and Craig had been in complete agreement about the value of independence when it was applied to their own behavior. But when it was applied to their children, they were in conflict.

Conflicting Values

When I have the opportunity to counsel a couple before they marry, I ask them to explain their values to each other. And I make a special point of asking them which of those values they plan to *teach* their children, particularly when it comes to religious education. If they have conflicting values, I encourage them to reach enthusiastic agreement on how they will educate their children.

In some cases, after trying to reach agreement, they discover that their positions seem non-negotiable. For example, a Catholic woman wants her children raised Catholic, and her Muslim fiancé wants the children trained in Islam. They may consider giving their children education in both religions, letting the kids make the final choice. But because most Catholics and Muslims believe that their respective religion is the only path to heaven, they are not really enthusiastic about that plan.

It's been my experience that people with conflicting values go into marriage with the hope that they can convert their spouse to their way of thinking. But if that hope is not realized, the conflicts that result seem irresolvable. Then when children come along, they fight over whose values will be taught to the kids.

> Deep down, Beth knew there was something wrong with trying to behave independently of others. And she was right.

But Beth and Craig thought they were in agreement regarding their basic value of independence—until it came to teaching it to their children. Beth's reluctance revealed the fact that she didn't really value it after all. Deep down, she knew there was something wrong with trying to behave independently of others. And she was right.

Independent behavior is one of the six Love Busters I introduced to you earlier. It's behaving as if others don't exist—it's thoughtless behavior. Since Craig felt that people couldn't really be trusted to care for him, why should he care for them? Instead of being thoughtful, Craig was inclined to use people to his advantage but not to their advantage—Beth included. And the more we talked about this implication, the more uncomfortable Beth became. They had not come to me for marriage counseling, but that's where we were headed before our first session was only half finished.

Craig was beginning to think he'd become too honest with Beth when he described his value of independence. He had never confessed that he didn't trust her before, but now the cat was out of the bag. His honesty was not a mistake, however. It was the first step toward solving a problem that would have ruined his marriage if left unattended.

So I went on to discover how Beth and Craig's value of independence had affected their marriage. It turned out that they were becoming like two ships passing in the night. If their romantic relationship and marriage were to be saved, they'd have to change their value from independence to interdependence.

Independence versus Interdependence

Beth and Craig had many reasons why they considered independent behavior essential for a healthy and happy marriage. Both had grown up trusting only themselves. And with no one else to trust, why consider anyone else's feelings? From their perspective, the only way to stay happily married was to give each other plenty of space—and the right to make whatever decisions each thought was appropriate for him or her. They made independent decisions and respected each other's right to independence.

But after only one year of marriage, their relationship was falling apart. Decisions that were appropriate for one of them were not necessarily appropriate for the other, and the creation of an incompatible lifestyle was well on its way to making them both miserable. They had developed separate friends and recreational interests, and they deposited their paychecks into their own checking accounts, spending their money as each of them saw fit. And since they were sales representatives for different companies, their work took them away from each other for days at a time.

Both of them ignored the fact that almost everything they did affected each other. While Beth and Craig thought they had the right to behave independently, they couldn't get away with it emotionally. The time they were away from each other, for both business and pleasure, cut deeply into their Love Bank accounts.

> Beth and Craig thought they had the right to behave independently, but they couldn't get away with it emotionally.

But if independent behavior didn't work for them in marriage, Craig knew that dependent behavior could be even worse. He saw what it had done to his mother, who found herself totally dependent on his alcoholic and unfaithful father. She was chronically depressed and seemed incapable of taking charge of her own life until his dad finally divorced her. Neither Beth nor Craig wanted any part of unhealthy dependence.

But as we've already seen, unhealthy dependence is not the only alternative to independence. A third alternative exists—interdependence, which is behaving in ways that simultaneously take our own feelings and the feelings of others into account.

Interdependence Is Thoughtfulness

In that first session with Beth and Craig, I set the stage for one of the most important values parents can teach their children—thoughtfulness. Independent behavior is thoughtless behavior, ignoring the interests of others, and dependent behavior is also thoughtless because it ignores your own interests. But interdependent behavior avoids the errors of both—it combines the interests of yourself and others. It's thoughtful because you think about others before you act, and you also consider your own interests.

> Thoughtfulness—it's one of the most important values that parents can teach their children.

Interdependence is much more than an important child-training value. It's a value that helps make marriages successful and fulfilling. I explained to Craig and Beth how almost everything they did made either deposits or withdrawals in their Love Banks. If they wanted a fulfilling marriage, they had to behave in ways that made each other happy and avoided making each other unhappy. I went on to show them how their independent behavior was almost certain to make sizable Love Bank withdrawals, but if they became interdependent, their behavior would make Love Bank deposits.

At first, Craig was skeptical that interdependence could work in their marriage. He felt that they were both so entrenched in independent behavior that a change might be too much to expect. But he agreed with me that interdependent behavior would be an improvement for him, if Beth were willing to make the change. All the money she earned had been going into her personal checking account, and she'd been spending it with little consideration for his concerns. She would make plans to go out with her friends without so much as mentioning it to him. And when she did choose to be home with him, she'd be on the telephone most of the evening, giving him very little of her time and attention.

These and a host of other examples of Beth's inconsiderate behavior made it very clear to Craig that more consideration on her part would definitely improve their relationship. But it was more difficult for him to understand how changes in his behavior would also improve their relationship. He didn't see his own thoughtlessness as that big a deal. Besides, if he were expected to give up his weekend golfing or to check with Beth every time he wanted to buy something for himself, he would feel trapped. That would not improve their relationship at all—it would end it as far as he was concerned.

But I explained that thoughtfulness was not a trap—it was an escape from what would become a very unfulfilling marriage for both of them. Being thoughtful didn't mean that Craig had to do whatever Beth demanded. It meant that he had to negotiate with Beth until they both agreed enthusiastically on what would be done.

Once Craig understood how they were both ruining their marriage by being independent, and how much their marriage would improve by being interdependent, he also began to see how crucial it was to teach their children thoughtfulness. The same advantages that interdependence would give their marriage would also benefit their children in their relationships with others.

The more we discussed the advantages of interdependence, the more Craig realized that all of his other child-training goals would be much more difficult to achieve without that value. He wanted his children to clean up after themselves, avoid fights with each other, and help around the house. All of those goals were instances of thoughtfulness and could be better understood by his children if they were taught to be considerate. And even doing well in school turns out to be an act of thoughtfulness, because academic preparation really does prepare people for a lifetime of care.

On the other hand, if Craig's children were raised to be independent, they'd learn to ignore the feelings of others. Why clean up their room if the mess doesn't bother them? And why avoid fights or help with chores or do well in school? They might do these things to avoid being punished, but not because they understood their value. And as they grew older and the threat of punishment ended, they'd have no reason to continue doing any of those things.

> If children are raised to be independent, they learn to ignore the feelings of others.

There were many other values that Beth and Craig could have discussed during this first session, but I only addressed the value of thoughtfulness. That's because most other values, such as honesty, ambition, patience, and dependability, are best understood in the context of this one value. Once it's taught, it's easier to explain the relevance of the others.

But there is one other value that you may have noticed missing in our discussion so far: religious faith. Since I have counseled those of many different faiths, I have left specific application of that value to parents.

However, I should mention that Joyce and I are Christians, which means that we value our relationship with Jesus Christ above everything else. As we raised our children, we wanted them to understand that there is nothing more important in life than that spiritual relationship. So as soon as they could talk, we taught them who Jesus Christ is, and how he was crucified and rose from the dead to save them from their sins. If they were to make him their Savior and Lord, they would have eternal life in heaven. Today, they have the same faith in Jesus as Joyce and I do—and so do their children. From our perspective, that's the most important value they could have learned.

By the time we had reached the end of the first session, Beth and Craig both agreed that an important goal in raising children is teaching them to be thoughtful. But how would they go about achieving that objective? More specifically, how would they use discipline, or punishment, in their efforts to train their children? That question would be answered in our second session.

Session 2 Child Discipline

I began session two with a very brief summary of the mental development of children. Infants (up to six months) begin life with very little understanding—all they understand is comfort and discomfort. They generally respond to comfort with a cheerful giggling and to discomfort with crying. It's cruel and pointless to discipline infants for crying, because they only do this in response to a need. When they are upset, they should be fed, held, diapered, put to sleep, or whatever else it takes to make them comfortable. Quite frankly, parents make a terrible mistake when they punish infants or even try to train them, because their ability to learn is so limited.

But it doesn't take long before a child can learn very simple rules of cause and effect. If young toddlers (six to twelve months) get what they want by crying, they learn to become real crybabies. So there's a point when discipline is not only appropriate but also crucial for the sanity of parents. However, the method of discipline should reflect the toddler's very limited learning capabilities and the sensitivities of both parents. Don't expect your toddler to obey complex spoken commands, and don't discipline him or her until you've reached an enthusiastic agreement on how you will do it.

Older toddlers (one to two years) can usually understand language and simple rules, so spoken commands begin to affect their behavior. But their cognitive ability cannot yet handle complex rules, such as caring for others. Some training objectives, such as toilet training, can be achieved at this age if a reward, like M&Ms, is given whenever the toddler performs the desired behavior. On the other hand, most forms of punishment for failing to use the toilet appropriately are cruel and ineffective. Punishment for dangerous acts, such as putting fingers in electric plug sockets or on hot ovens, can be effective, but the general principles behind such dangers cannot yet be fully understood.

Preschool-age children (three to four) are still too young for complex concepts, but it doesn't hurt to introduce some of them in the form of games and bedtime stories. Most children's games and books are value oriented, so be sure to choose the ones that support the specific values you want your children to learn. Although the principles may not be fully grasped at the time, when a child becomes a teenager, those memories will suddenly make sense. As the Book of Proverbs reminds us, "Train a child in the way he should go, and when he is old he will not turn from it" (22:6).

> Training methods should change as children develop greater ability to understand complex rules.

As the child's brain grows and assimilates experiences, simple rules of behavior develop into more complex rules. And thoughtfulness is one of the most complex rules of all. The ability to fully understand this rule is only possible very late in a child's development (ages eleven to fourteen), and it assumes a sophisticated awareness of how the child's own behavior affects the pleasure and pain of others. But as I mentioned, the basic principles of thoughtfulness should be explained early in a child's life, even though he or she should not be expected to fully grasp its meaning.

Training methods should change as children develop greater ability to understand complex rules. What works for toddlers doesn't work as well for preschool children, and what works for preschoolers doesn't work as well for early school children. By the time a child reaches sixteen, if his or her parents are still using training methods that are only appropriate for younger children, they often lose their influence entirely. What they blame on teenage rebellion is often the fault of training methods not appropriate for that age.

A Discipline Dilemma

When I finished giving Beth and Craig this brief course on the mental development of children, and how discipline should change with their age, I introduced an issue that was sure to become a conflict—child discipline. I asked them both to explain to me how they planned to punish their children.

It didn't take long before the conflict became apparent. Beth wanted to avoid punishment entirely, because she had suffered so much abuse by her mother. Besides, she was afraid that if she punished her children at all, the floodgates would open and she would turn out to be abusive, just like her mother had been.

Craig, on the other hand, felt that punishment was necessary to get a child's attention. When he was growing up, punishment had helped keep him in line.

To help Beth and Craig come to an agreement regarding discipline, I told them about another couple I had counseled, Alex and Christine.

Alex had a short fuse. His friends and family all knew it. But when he fell in love with Christine, he cared so much for her that he managed to keep his temper under control whenever he was with her. Christine became his bride because of his victory over this ugly Love Buster. And their marriage went well because he kept his vow never to subject her to his angry outbursts. He never punished her either verbally or physically.

However, he'd been brought up in a tradition in which heavy-handed discipline was considered the father's duty. When Alex was a child, his father had beaten him on many occasions—if he disobeyed, he could expect disastrous consequences. And Alex had learned first-hand about those disastrous consequences.

When Alex and Christine had their first child, Alex expected the same unwavering obedience that his parents had expected of him. Whenever little Matthew misbehaved, Alex disciplined him the way *he* had been disciplined as a child.

Christine became increasingly upset with the way Matthew was being punished and finally went to her pastor for help. But the pastor recommended that she leave the discipline up to her husband, giving her examples of children who grew up to be criminals because women raised them without a father's punishment.

The pastor's advice did more harm than good. Alex had actually been holding back his temper somewhat because he realized how it affected Christine. But now that he had his pastor's permission to do whatever he felt was right regarding discipline, he released all his pent-up fury on young Matthew. Whenever he felt irritated about something, he punished his son.

All the while, Alex was careful never to treat Christine abusively. In fact, he went out of his way to be sure she understood that his punishment of Matthew was a father's responsibility, something that had to be done. But still she suffered every time he punished the child, crying as if he were punishing her. Even though Alex had shown her exceptional care in other ways, this punishment caused huge withdrawals from her Love Bank, to say nothing about how it was scarring Matthew emotionally.

Two Heads Are Better Than One

In my experience counseling families, I've found that every couple's joint methods of discipline are superior to their individual methods. Couples are wiser in the way they train their children when they agree on a training method. By discussing options and agreeing on a particular approach, they eliminate many of the foolish and impulsive acts of discipline that either one of them might try individually. And children take their parents more seriously when both parents agree on an approach.

> A couple's joint methods of discipline are superior to their individual methods.

So my first step in helping Alex and Christine resolve their conflict was to encourage them to agree on a method of discipline before using it. Of course, this was a radical departure from what their pastor had recommended. But since it was the pastor himself who had suggested they counsel with me, Alex was willing to try it. That one decision put an end to the abuse Alex had inflicted on his son, because Christine had never been in favor of it.

But they had to do more than just stop Alex's abusive behavior. They had to discover an alternative method of discipline that they could agree to use enthusiastically. That's when they put the Four Guidelines for Successful Negotiation into action.

In spite of his bad temper, Alex had learned to protect Christine from it—he never vented his anger against her. So he already knew how to follow the first guideline, making their negotiations pleasant and safe.

The second guideline, identifying the problem from both of their perspectives, was also fairly easy to accomplish. Christine had explained to Alex on many occasions that she wanted him to focus more attention on Matthew's good behavior than on his bad behavior. She wanted him to reward his son far more than he punished him. And she wanted the punishment to be nonviolent—taking away privileges rather than physical beatings or verbal assaults.

Alex had also explained his perspective to Christine many times in the past. He felt that children had to be severely punished or they would eventually run wild. And he felt that the pastor of his church and verses in the Bible supported his belief. He read Proverbs 13:24 to Christine: "He who spares the rod hates his son, but he who loves him is careful to discipline him." He loved Matthew and felt that his discipline was a necessary part of raising him correctly.

But he also loved Christine and knew that the way he was disciplining Matthew was tearing her heart in two. And as he reflected on his own childhood, he began to see how the physical beatings he had endured were unnecessarily brutal. The more he thought about it, the more he knew it was not the way he should have been raised.

By the time they understood and respected each other's perspectives, Alex and Christine were ready for the third guideline—brainstorming. How could Matthew be disciplined in a way that would meet the goal of the Policy of Joint Agreement—mutual enthusiastic agreement?

While they were brainstorming, Alex understood that he could do nothing if Matthew was disobedient. That's because they had not yet agreed on an appropriate response. So Alex had extra incentive to quickly find an alternative to his abusive methods. And within a week, they both had agreed enthusiastically on an experimental plan. They were to put some of Christine's ideas into practice, focusing more attention on Matthew's good behavior than on his bad behavior. And they also agreed to nonviolent forms of punishment—no more physical beatings or verbal assaults.

When Alex and Christine came to an enthusiastic agreement on discipline, Alex's abuse was eliminated and his relationship with Christine was restored. The Policy of Joint Agreement helped Alex end the chain of violence that had plagued his family for generations.

Child Training's Golden Rule

After describing Alex and Christine's case to Beth and Craig, I suggested a few general rules of discipline that they should follow. The first rule is that punishment should decrease with age. It's most effective during preschool years, somewhat effective up to the age of ten, and usually ineffective after puberty. That's why parents who punish their teenage children usually find themselves in battles they can't win. Joyce and I eliminated punishment entirely when our children reached the age of twelve.

A second general rule of discipline is that rewards should be given far more often than punishments, even for small children. And as children grow, the ratio of rewards to punishments should increase—more rewards, fewer punishments.

And a third rule to follow is that your training should teach children to be thoughtful. Whatever it is that you reward or punish should be an instance of that overarching goal. By teaching your children to consider the feelings of others, you have a basic rationale for a host of more specific training goals.

> Your children will learn the most by watching how you treat each other.

But the golden rule of discipline is that your own behavior is your most effective training tool. Your children will learn the most by watching how you treat each other. While training methods and the appropriateness of punishment change with age, the effectiveness of your example doesn't change. So you should show your children how to behave by behaving that way yourselves.

Children will not likely pick up their toys if the kitchen is always a mess. They won't learn to avoid fighting if they see their parents fight. And they'll resist helping around the house unless they see their parents helping each other. "Do as I say, not as I do" is a very ineffective training rule. If you want your children to grow up to be thoughtful, you must also be considerate of each other's feelings.

I explained to Beth and Craig that now was the time for them to practice setting a good example for the child they were about to have. Now was the time for them to learn to be thoughtful. I challenged Beth and Craig to get into the habit of asking each other how they felt about literally everything they did. It seemed silly to them at first, because so much of what they did was regarded as personal—even private. But they had read enough about the Policy of Joint Agreement to understand the importance of mutual agreement. And they understood that the question "How do you feel about . . ." gets the ball rolling, so they were willing to try.

Have you and your spouse given the Policy of Joint Agreement a chance to revolutionize your own marriage? If not, much more than your relationship may be suffering—you probably haven't created good habits to demonstrate to your children. After all, how can you teach thoughtfulness to your children if you aren't thoughtful to each other?

> How can you teach thoughtfulness to your children if you aren't thoughtful to each other?

I give you the same advice I gave Beth and Craig—put the Policy of Joint Agreement into practice now. They had the advantage of practicing it before they had their first child. But if yours have already arrived, it's not too late to change the course of your lives. It will help keep your Love Banks full, and as your children watch your care for each other, thoughtfulness will become a way of life for your whole family.

The Time Factor

Practicing the Policy of Undivided Attention

What are the two most important characteristics of good parents? We've just discussed one of them—making all child-rearing decisions with mutual agreement. But there's another characteristic that is equally important. Do you know what it is?

The answer, of course, is being in love with each other. When parents are in love, their marriage is secure—there's no risk of divorce, which is one of the worst things parents can do to their children. Unfortunately, many parents spend so much of their time perfecting the first characteristic—making wise parenting decisions—that they neglect the second—being in love.

But even if children are taught the most important values and are raised with the wisest forms of discipline, when parents are not in love, the entire family is at risk of annihilation. That's because being out of love is the primary cause of divorce. Besides, it's essentially impossible for parents to set the best examples of thoughtfulness when they are not in love with each other.

When parents are not in
love, the entire family is
at risk of annihilation.

So when I counsel couples in parenting skills, I explain how important it is for them to guard their love for each other. And if they've lost that love, I show them how to restore it, because it's an essential ingredient for their children's happiness. After two sessions with Beth and Craig, we had come to this issue. Were they in love with each other? And if so, how would they guarantee their love after the baby arrived?

Session 3 Romance in Marriage

My first two counseling sessions with Beth and Craig had taken them through some very important territory. We'd addressed the issues of values and discipline—crucial topics for parents. And decisions were made during those sessions that would greatly improve their parenting skills. By following the Policy of Joint Agreement, they would become wiser in the way they raised their children, and they would also set an example of thoughtfulness.

But the best was yet to come. We would now address the issue of love.

Beth and Craig had drifted apart during their first year of marriage. They were creating independent lifestyles that not only were thoughtless but also gave them very little time to meet each other's important emotional needs. And I knew what that could do to their Love Bank balances. I was almost certain that their accounts had fallen below the romantic love threshold.

To confirm my suspicions, I asked them to complete my twenty-one-item Love Bank Inventory, a test that measures the feeling of love. When they were finished, I quickly scored the tests, and the results showed that neither of them was in love. Without revealing their scores, I asked them to explain what they did together prior to marriage. Beth described what most couples do—they had made a special effort to be together almost daily, and they used that time to meet each other's intimate emotional needs. That required a careful scheduling of their time.

Then I asked them to describe what they did together now that they were married. Craig admitted that they were no longer setting aside time to be together, and their intimate emotional needs were not being met. They both knew something was wrong but didn't know how to fix it. Like so many other newlyweds, they were trying to take shortcuts.

Beth wanted Craig to talk with her more often and to be more affectionate but wasn't as motivated to join him in his recreational interests or be sexually responsive to him. Craig, on the other hand, wanted Beth to spend more recreational time with him and make love more often but wasn't as willing to spend as much time talking to her or showing as much affection as he had in the past. Since marriage, they had cut back on meeting each other's intimate emotional needs so that they could devote more time to their personal goals and interests, and the results were beginning to show.

> They both knew something was wrong but didn't know how to fix it.

I asked Beth and Craig to explain what it was to be in love and what it takes to sustain that feeling. Having just taken my Love Bank Inventory, they guessed correctly that the items they answered helped define the feeling of love, so they tried to remember what they were.

"When you're in love, you overlook mistakes—you're not as critical. And you feel like making love all the time," Craig replied. Those were the items on the test that impressed him the most.

"It's a chemistry—you're very attracted to each other. You bring the best out of each other when you're in love," was Beth's response.

"Now tell me what a romantic relationship is," I said.

"It's when people are in love," Beth replied, and Craig agreed.

"But is a romantic relationship just a feeling? Don't you do something when you're in a romantic relationship?" I probed.

"You do what comes naturally—you spend time together, you cuddle, you talk to each other a lot . . . you know, you express your love to each other," Beth answered.

"Could you be in a romantic relationship without expressing your love?" I asked.

"It sure wouldn't be very romantic." Craig could see where I was headed. "So I suppose we haven't had much of a romantic relationship lately."

"You got that one right!" Beth blurted out.

That's when I gave them my definition of a romantic relationship—two people in love who meet each other's intimate emotional needs. I explained that they could not have a romantic relationship unless both parts of the definition were true. They had to be in love *and* be meeting each other's intimate emotional needs.

Craig and Beth already knew how to meet these intimate emotional needs for each other but had neglected to schedule the time to do it. And their attempts at shortcuts didn't work—they just made them more frustrated.

So I challenged them to schedule fifteen hours each week to meet those emotional needs. I suggested they meet at 3:30 every Sunday afternoon to look over each other's schedule for the coming week, and I gave them the Time for Undivided Attention Work Sheet (appendix B) to document the time they spent meeting each other's intimate emotional needs. I warned them that planned time wouldn't match up with actual time unless undivided attention was their highest priority. Before marriage they had been careful not to stand each other up on dates, and I explained that the time they scheduled now was to be considered a date.

I also wanted them to check their schedules on Sunday afternoon to be sure that everything in them followed the Policy of Joint Agreement. Were they planning their week with mutual agreement or were they reverting to their independent lifestyles? They were to ask each other how they felt about everything they planned to do. If one was not enthusiastic about what was planned, they were to negotiate a mutual agreement.

I encouraged Beth and Craig to get into the habit of asking each other how they felt about everything they did. If one of them were to object, they were to use the Four Guidelines for Successful Negotiation to resolve the conflict. This thoughtfulness for each other now would prepare them to set an example of thoughtfulness for their children.

But Beth and Craig had a long way to go. Getting into the habit of negotiating successfully in marriage would take them weeks, if not months. Fortunately, they had a few months to learn that important skill before their first child arrived.

As our session came to a close, I suggested that they practice following the Policy of Joint Agreement and the Policy of Undivided Attention for six consecutive weeks before their next appointment. And if they ran into any serious problems or missed spending fifteen hours together during a week, they should call me for a brief emergency telephone session.

Session 4 How to Keep Children from Threatening Your Love

Six weeks after my third session with Beth and Craig, they were back in my office for their next appointment—and they definitely had the look of love. But just to be certain, I had them complete the Love Bank Inventory again in my office. Their scores were very high this time.

During my thirty-five years of counseling, one of my most rewarding experiences has been to witness couples falling back in love with each other. In most cases, it takes more than six weeks, but Beth and Craig's Love Bank balances had not fallen very far, and they had not forgotten how to meet each other's intimate emotional needs.

They showed me the Time for Undivided Attention Work Sheets they had completed, and I could see why they were now so much in love. Their first week was rough—they barely made it to their goal of fifteen hours and didn't enjoy their time together that much. But the second week was much better, and eventually they were back to meeting each other's intimate emotional needs the way they had in the past.

When that happened, they had no problem scheduling time for undivided attention. In fact, by the sixth week they were spending about twenty-five hours with each other. It's something that couples can do without much effort if they don't have children. And if you're in love, it's easier to find time to be with each other.

If you're in love, it's easier to find time to be with each other.

During those six weeks, they learned that if they stopped meeting each other's intimate emotional needs and started making thoughtless decisions, they would lose their feeling of love. But they also learned that when they met those needs and made thoughtful decisions, their love would be restored. It was one of the most important object lessons they could have experienced—their love for each other depended on care and consideration.

Personal Schedules and the Policy of Joint Agreement

I had asked Beth and Craig to bring their personal schedules with them so I could see how they spent all their time each week. Their schedules included the time they set aside for undivided attention, but I wanted to see everything else they planned to do. After they handed them to me, I gave Beth's to Craig and Craig's to Beth. "Are you enthusiastic about what you see?" I asked.

If I had asked that question six weeks earlier, there would have been plenty of complaints. But their effort to follow the Policy of Joint Agreement and spend time giving each other undivided attention had eliminated most of them. Instead of playing golf all day Saturday with his friends, Craig was now playing golf with Beth. And Beth had suspended her morning workout at the health club to exercise with Craig instead.

But they were still making some scheduling decisions without discussing them with each other. For example, Beth was not at all enthusiastic about Craig's working lunch with Rachel, an attractive product manager for his company. But she had not said anything about it because she felt it was part of his job.

The Policy of Joint Agreement is more difficult to follow when your spouse objects to what seems to be a career requirement. Craig's boss was the one who suggested that he have lunch with Rachel each week so he could give her information about new products without taking time away from his other responsibilities. The policy also can be difficult to follow when you're in love and want your spouse to have whatever makes him or her happy. Now that Beth was in love with Craig again, she was more reluctant to object to anything that he was doing.

That's why I stress *enthusiastic* agreement. Reluctant agreement in marriage can establish some very unhealthy habits, but enthusiastic agreement makes these habits almost impossible to form.

If Craig had asked Beth, "How would you feel if I had lunch with Rachel today?" she might have given her approval reluctantly. But if he had asked again, "Are you enthusiastic about it?" he would have heard a different answer. They both understood how important it was to develop good habits, so after their session with me, Craig told his boss he needed to have lunch in peace so he could relax, which was definitely the truth. He asked if he could schedule his meetings with Rachel on company time, with other employees present, and his boss agreed.

The Policy of Undivided Attention and the Policy of Joint Agreement work together to keep Love Bank balances high. The one helps make Love Bank deposits with the meeting of intimate emotional needs, and the other helps prevent Love Bank withdrawals by short-circuiting thoughtlessness. Together they guarantee a lifetime of love in spite of life's twists and turns—and in spite of children.

> The Policy of Undivided Attention and the Policy of Joint Agreement work together to guarantee a lifetime of love in spite of life's twists and turns and in spite of children.

Learning to follow these policies also provides the example that children need. As parents become increasingly skilled in negotiating with each other, they are able to teach the value of thoughtfulness with their own behavior.

How Children Change Your Schedules

If Beth and Craig were to stay in love with each other, they would not only have to continue scheduling time to meet each other's intimate emotional needs, they would also have to make all of their scheduling decisions with enthusiastic agreement.

But their future children would not make it easy for them to spend time alone. They would want as much of their parents' attention as possible. Yet unless Beth and Craig protected their time for undivided attention at all costs, their love for each other would be lost. When their first child finally arrived, their commitment to the Policy of Undivided Attention would really be put to the test.

They were now in a great position to consider how children might affect the way they cared for each other. By factoring kids into their lives, it would be easy to understand how they might neglect each other's intimate emotional needs.

> The primary responsibility for child training should remain with parents, whether or not they have dual careers.

How much time *does* a child require? Well, it depends on the age of the child and the decisions parents make about how to handle child-care tasks. If you are like most families, in which both spouses continue their careers after children arrive, I strongly recommend getting help from nonparental custodians—day-care providers, in-home babysitters, and various combinations of relatives and friends—to help out with some of the child-care tasks when needed. When a husband and wife both work, many tasks commonly associated with child care can be delegated to others without any risk of harming the development of the child.

But I draw a distinction between child care and child training. The primary responsibility for child training should remain with parents, whether or not they have dual careers.

With child training in mind, I encourage parents to set aside time for it each week—I call it **Quality Family Time**. This is not child care—it's child training. It's when the family is together for the expressed purpose of teaching children the value of thoughtfulness. This time would include teaching them to clean up after themselves, avoid fights with each other, help with chores, and do well in school. But these and other common child-training goals all would be taught as examples of thoughtfulness. This training would take place while you are having meals together, going out for walks and bike rides, playing games, watching videos, attending church services, reading books together, praying before bedtime, and working on family projects.

As Beth and Craig looked at their schedules, they tried to imagine where they would find time for just the basic care a child would require. To add quality family time—time for child training—seemed utterly impossible. "How does a guy feel when you drop this idea on him after he has three kids?" Craig asked. "He's working overtime to pay the bills, spends his evenings and weekends feeding and diapering babies, and when he gets a break, fixes things around the house. There's no time for a little relaxation, let alone quality family time."

"Is that what you're afraid your life will become?" I asked.

"It's occurred to me," he responded.

"A sensible schedule solves that problem," was my answer.

Don't Add Responsibilities—Replace Them

As I mentioned when we were discussing how to find time for undivided attention, a new responsibility, like quality family time, should not be *added* to existing responsibilities—it should *replace* some of them.

There are only so many hours in a week, and we have only so much energy. So when we find ourselves overwhelmed with responsibilities, we must prioritize them and eliminate the ones that are least valuable to us. A week consists of 168 hours—7 24-hour days. If you sleep 8 hours a day, that leaves you 112 waking hours. An hour to take a shower and have breakfast in the morning (7 hours), about half an hour to get to and from work on weekdays (3 hours), and about 15 minutes to get ready for bed each night (2 hours) leaves 100 hours.

If you work 50 hours a week (including lunch and other breaks) and schedule 15 hours for undivided attention and another 15 hours for Quality Family Time with your children, you still have 20 hours a week remaining for everything else you consider important in life, including relaxation. In other words, if you think 15 hours for quality family time is too much time, remember that you have even more time available each week for whatever else you think is important.

> Quality family time should not be *added* to existing responsibilities—it should *replace* some of them.

And you can increase your total time for relaxation by achieving two objectives at once. If your dinner is with your family, it can be part of your quality family time. Cooking the dinner and cleaning up afterward can also be included as quality family time if you do it together as a family. And attending church services together as a family would certainly qualify, if you were personally involved in helping your children learn the lessons being taught.

In another example of combining objectives, your time spent with your spouse or family can definitely be included as part of your leisure time each week. Time for undivided attention and quality family time can be very relaxing if you plan things right. And with twenty hours left over for anything else you consider important, there's still time to just vegetate if that's what you want to do.

Budgeting your time is as important as budgeting your money. Without a financial budget you will tend to spend your limited resources on low priority items, finding yourself broke when high priority items come due. The same is true with time. If you don't schedule your time, you will waste much of it on responsibilities that are of little value to you, leaving you exhausted when it's time to fulfill more important responsibilities.

The reason that most dual-career parents, especially mothers, are tired most of the time is because they don't get enough sleep. They make their own health a lower priority than less important objectives. Instead of budgeting their time wisely, they do whatever seems urgent, and there is no end to it.

Housework and child care are the culprits for most working mothers. They wake up in the morning, making breakfast for their children and getting them dressed and ready for school, and then after a long day at work, they have dinner to prepare and piles of laundry waiting to be washed and ironed. Husbands are usually some help, but not nearly enough—they have exhausting days too.

To avoid exhaustion while raising your family, you should do what I encouraged Beth and Craig to do—start planning a weekly schedule together every Sunday afternoon at 3:30. Write down everything, including morning showers and breakfast. You should not work more than fifty hours, and you should plan a minimum of fifteen hours for undivided attention and another fifteen hours for quality family time. And don't forget eight hours of sleep every night. The time remaining should take into account how much energy you have left. Who will prepare meals, do the laundry, clean the bathrooms, vacuum the rugs, and wash the windows?

> Budgeting your time is as important as budgeting your money.

Parents should divide their household and child-care responsibilities fairly so that neither spouse is burning the candle at both ends. I didn't have time during our fourth session to explain how to create a fair division of labor, so I gave Craig and Beth reading material and work sheets that explain how it's to be done. In the next chapter, I will describe that important procedure to you.

But for now I simply want you to be aware of the fact that far too many parents are trying to do too much these days. And the culprit is their schedules. If you budget time with your highest priorities in mind, you will find yourselves with plenty of energy to do what's most important—meeting each other's intimate emotional needs, training your children to be happy and successful adults, maintaining a productive career, and completing necessary household and child-care tasks.

Granted, there are many parents who are not willing to change their priorities. These are the exhausted parents who neglect their

children and each other—to say nothing about their own health. If
your schedule is too full for fifteen hours a week of undivided attention and fifteen hours a week for quality
family time, I warn you: You risk failing
at both marriage and parenting. Look at
everything you are doing each week and
ask yourself this question: Are these things
really more important than my spouse and
my children? Unless you change your priorities so that your family comes first in
your life, your health, career, and everything else you value will suffer.

> If your schedule is
> too full for fifteen
> hours a week of
> undivided attention and
> fifteen hours a week for
> quality family time, I
> warn you You risk failing
> at both marriage and
> parenting.

By the end of the fourth session, Beth
and Craig knew how they could keep
romance in their marriage after children
arrived. Regardless of the added pressure
that a child would create, they could keep
their romantic relationship secure simply by taking time to meet each
other's intimate emotional needs.

But the schedule would do more than keep them in love with each
other. It would also make their lifestyles much more compatible. By
working out each week's schedule together and using the Policy of
Joint Agreement to make decisions as to how every hour was spent,
they both would be happy with the way the week unfolded. They
would be interdependent.

We had one more session to go, and I wanted to use it to hold
them accountable for the changes they'd promised to make for each
other. And I also wanted to answer any questions they would have
regarding scheduling problems.

Their final assignment was to continue meeting at 3:30 on Sunday afternoons to create a schedule for each week. Two copies were
to be made so each of them would know what the other was doing.
And if there was a change in schedule, they were to ask if the change
would be okay.

They also were to continue meeting each other's intimate emotional needs, but I didn't think I had to make it an assignment—by that time they were on autopilot.

Since I wanted to give them time to form the habit of scheduling their week together, my final appointment with them was set three months away, just before the birth of their new baby. But I told them that if they stopped scheduling their week together or stopped meeting each other's emotional needs, they should call me for an emergency telephone session.

Session 5 Time for Kids?

When Beth and Craig returned for their fifth and final session three months later, they began by telling me that Ann's gift of five parenting sessions was the best anniversary gift they could have received. Their marriage had been in deeper trouble than they'd realized, and the emphasis I placed on interdependence and meeting intimate emotional needs was what was needed to get it back on track.

They had read my materials regarding a fair division of labor (you'll read them in the next chapter) and tried to apply it to their present household responsibilities. Although they knew their life was much simpler now than it would be with children, they were able to see light at the end of the tunnel. By dividing child-care and household responsibilities with thoughtfulness, they began to see how the arrival of children could be an exciting and fulfilling adventure instead of an exhausting mistake.

They also had a much clearer understanding of what quality family time would require. After completing a reading assignment on the subject and discussing it with each other, they began to see how they would train their children—training they had missed when they were growing up.

If they had continued on the independent paths they were taking, having a child probably would have ended their marriage. They would have made parenting decisions the way they'd been making all of their decisions—independently. And instead of finding solutions that made them both happy, they would have demanded solutions that worked for only one of them. In the end, they would have made each other miserable, and divorce would've been almost inevitable.

But even if they'd managed to remain married, they wouldn't have been good parents because of their independent behavior. They would have set an example for their children to be inconsiderate of others—that's the way they treated each other.

By the end of my last session with Beth and Craig, they were ready for their first child. And within a few weeks, I received an announcement of the birth of their new daughter, Ashley.

10

His Work, Her Work

How to Divide Domestic Responsibilities

I t's tragic but true that the first baby often sinks a marriage. You'd think it would be the other way around, that a baby would draw a husband and wife closer together. But there are good reasons why children in general, and babies in particular, can make marriages worse rather than better.

Part of the problem is something I've mentioned many times in this book. When a couple becomes parents, they often stop being lovers—they no longer meet each other's intimate emotional needs.

But there's another reason why a first child can threaten a marriage—flawed approaches to problem solving. Before children arrive, a couple can get away with unwise decisions because their lives are relatively simple and stress-free. But their first child puts an end to simplicity. And along with the new complexities of life, new lifestyle decisions can have almost immediate consequences. Wise decisions mean life with a new baby can be great, but unwise decisions send spouses diving for cover.

A Frustrated Mom

Amy was suffering the consequences of unwise decisions. The arrival of her first child proved it—she was very frustrated. So she sent this letter to me asking for my advice.

Dear Dr. Harley,

I have a three-month-old son, Ryan, who I love so much that I'm having mixed feelings about going back to work full time. I'd like to find something part time or work at home if possible. My husband, Ed, is now bearing the stress of only one income coming into the house, and sometimes he drives me crazy with his constant complaining about money.

I'm getting to the point where I am starting to resent him. I want to know if this is normal when you have one working partner and the other partner is currently staying at home to take care of the baby. I lose my patience with him and I also get mad that when he comes home, he only plays with the baby a little bit and then gives him to me to hold or calm down. I've tried explaining to him that when he comes home, it feels good for someone else to take care of the baby so I can do other things, like take a shower or watch TV. I don't know if I am into a type of postpartum depression or what, but I need some input on why I'm starting to resent him.

Amy

Ed apparently felt justified in turning over child-care responsibilities to Amy as long as he was the sole breadwinner in the family. But his analysis of the situation got him into lots of trouble because it didn't consider Amy's feelings. And Amy's decision to delay returning to her full-time job may not have considered Ed's feelings.

The wisest way for them to solve this problem, of course, would have been to come to an enthusiastic agreement regarding the division of their child-care responsibilities and Amy's return to work. And they should have come to that agreement before Ryan was born, with some fine-tuning after his arrival.

But if Ed and Amy were like most couples, they would have had trouble dividing child-care responsibilities even if Amy had gone right back to work. She would have expected Ed to put equal time into Ryan's care, and he would have resisted sharing the load. Most new working mothers find that their husbands' help isn't nearly enough.

Traditionally, wives have assumed most household and child-care responsibilities, while husbands have provided most of the income for the family. When couples could afford it, housekeepers and nannies lived in the home to take the burden of those responsibilities off the wife's shoulders.

> Most women try to do it all at first and then end up demanding help from their husbands.

But today, at least here in America, there are very few live-in housekeepers and nannies, and women are much more committed to careers outside of the home. That combination of factors makes husbands the most obvious resource to fill the gap. And while men are changing the diapers, wielding the mop, and tending to the stove more often than ever before, it usually isn't enough to compensate for their wives' career responsibilities. In dual-career marriages, men on average do less than half as much child care and housework as their wives.

At first, most women try to do it all. They wake up to dress children and make breakfast and then rush off to work. After a hard day at the office, they come home to find the house a mess and everybody wanting dinner. The evening is spent cleaning up, doing laundry, and finally dropping off to sleep after the last child is put to bed.

Does that routine sound fair to you? Most working women don't think so, and they usually demand more help from their husbands. But as we've already seen, demands don't get the job done. They lead to less, not more, compliance from a spouse.

Although Amy didn't mention it in her letter, my guess is that she had already tried making demands, and it didn't work. Instead, it was causing her to be even more frustrated by Ed's reluctant response.

A Fair Division of Labor

Are you and your spouse feeling overwhelmed with household chores and child care? And are you feeling frustrated because you aren't getting the help you need? The most sensible way to break out of this nightmare is to divide your household and child-care responsibilities in a way that both of you can agree to enthusiastically. Is that possible? Absolutely.

But what's equally important to understand is that demands, disrespectful judgments, or angry outbursts won't work. Try as you may to force each other to do the right thing, you will fail. The only way to succeed is to divide your responsibilities in a way that leads to an

SOUND FAMILIAR?

"Kevin, I need this house picked up before I get home from my meeting tonight," Melissa demanded as she grabbed her car keys. "Emily's birthday party is tomorrow night, and you haven't done a thing to help me get ready for it."

When she got home later that night, Melissa saw that her messy house hadn't changed a bit. "Kevin!" she yelled with dismay. "Do I have to do *everything* around here, or do you suppose you could stop being lazy for just fifteen minutes and help me out for a change?"

enthusiastic agreement. And that requires taking each other's feelings into account—mutual thoughtfulness.

It's worth a try, you may be thinking, *but how do we actually do it?*

Step 1: Identify your household and child-care responsibilities.

If you haven't yet had your first child, you may not be fully aware of everything that's involved. You may need the advice of your friends who already have children before you can identify every task you are likely to face once your baby arrives.

But if you already have children, the first step in agreeing to a fair division of labor is simply to list every domestic task you either find yourself doing or wanting your spouse to do. And the list should not just describe child care. It should also include other household tasks.

> The first step in agreeing to a fair division of labor is simply to list every domestic task.

As you identify each domestic task, (1) name the task, (2) briefly describe what must be done and when it should be accomplished, (3) identify the spouse who wants it accomplished, and (4) rate how important it is to that spouse. (Use a scale from 0 to 5, with 0 indicating not important and 5 indicating most important.)

Both of you should identify household tasks independently of each other throughout the day and then write them in your master list every evening. Add items to your list as you find yourself accomplishing various tasks or wanting them accomplished. It will take you several days to cover the bases.

Each time a task is added to this list, the spouse wanting it done should rate the task's importance. But the other spouse also must consider to what extent he or she would want it accomplished. So the importance ratings of both spouses should eventually accompany each item.

Here's an example of the list Amy and Ed might have started:

Task	Description	Who Named It?	Amy's Rating	Ed's Rating
Bathing and dressing Ryan in the morning	• getting him out of his crib by 7:00 • preparing his bath • disposing of his diaper • giving him a bath and shampoo • drying him and applying powder • dressing him for the day by 7:30	Amy	5	4
Cleaning the house	• dusting and vacuuming the living room and bedrooms • mopping floors in the kitchen and bathroom • wiping down counters and fixtures in the kitchen and bathroom	Amy	4	3
Preparing dinner	• planning a menu in advance of dinner • cooking dinner • setting the table • serving dinner at 6:00 or at another time mutually agreed upon	Ed	3	4

When you've finished your list, both of you should be satisfied that it includes all of the housekeeping and child-care tasks that you are presently accomplishing or wanting your spouse to accomplish. You may have as many as a hundred items listed. This part of the exercise alone will help you understand what you're up against with regard to the work that must be done.

Step 2: Assume responsibility for tasks that you would enjoy doing or prefer doing yourself.

Now comes the hard part—who will be responsible for the items you've both listed? You'll need to make two new lists to help you keep your assignments straight, one titled "His Responsibilities" and the other titled "Her Responsibilities."

Among the tasks you've listed, there will be some that you would enjoy doing, don't mind doing, or want to do by yourself so they can be done a certain way. Select those tasks from the master list and place them on your personal list. Each task you add to one of the new lists should be crossed off the original list.

If both you and your spouse want to take responsibility for the same tasks, you can either take turns doing them or arbitrarily divide them between the two of you. But you must approve each other's selections before they become your final responsibilities. If one of you doesn't feel that the other will perform the task well enough, you might give each other a trial period to demonstrate competence. Once you've taken responsibility for any task, your spouse should be able to hold you accountable for doing it according to his or her expectations.

> When you assume responsibilities, take into account how much time you have in your schedule to do them.

When you assume these responsibilities, take into account how much time you have in your schedule to do them. Don't take more than you have time to complete. And remember that your time for undivided attention must be preserved at all costs, so don't agree to do anything that would crowd it out. You will be tempted to consider your time together to be a luxury now that you have the responsibilities of children. But it's not a luxury—it's a necessity if you want your children to have parents who love each other.

And also don't forget to include quality family time. It's not child care. It's child training, and it should be included in your weekly schedule. In the next chapter, we'll discuss what to do with that time, but for now, I want you to simply acknowledge it.

When you've completed this second step, you'll have three lists: (1) the husband's list of responsibilities, (2) the wife's list of responsibilities, and (3) the list of household and child-care tasks that are not yet assigned.

Here's a look at part of the new list Ed and Amy might have created:

Amy's Responsibilities	Ed's Responsibilities	Unassigned
• Bathe and dress Ryan M–F • Plan meal menus for week • Cook and serve dinner on Monday through Thursday • Dust living room and bedrooms	• Bathe and dress Ryan on weekends • Cook and serve dinner on Sunday • Vacuum living room and bedrooms	• Cook and serve dinner on Friday and Saturday • Mop kitchen and bathroom floors. • Wipe down counters and fixtures in kitchen and bathroom.

Step 3: Assign the remaining tasks to the one wanting each done the most, or to someone hired to do them. Otherwise, eliminate them from your list.

Assuming that the tasks you wouldn't mind doing have been assigned to either the husband's list or the wife's list, you are left with those that neither of you wants to do but at least one of you thinks should be done.

At this point, some people choke on my next recommendation: I suggest that these unpleasant tasks be assigned to the person who wants them done the most, or to someone you hire. Otherwise, they should be eliminated from your list.

"But why should I get stuck doing more chores just because my husband is sloppy and doesn't care about keeping the house clean?" a wife may ask. "And why should I have to balance the checkbook all the time just because my wife thinks it's a waste of time?" a husband might reply.

I think it's the only reasonable solution. Why force responsibility of a task on the one who doesn't care if it's done? And how likely is it that they'll follow through if they have no motivation? The one most motivated to complete a task is the one who wants it done the most.

"But what if I don't have time to do anything more?" a wife might ask. "I've already committed myself to tasks that fill my schedule, but my lazy husband still has plenty of time left over. Why shouldn't he do a fair share of the work?"

Remember, what's fair to you isn't necessarily fair to your spouse. Just because he happens to have time in his schedule doesn't mean he wants to fill it with tasks he feels are needless. Besides, he may not regard his free time as empty. He may want it in his schedule every day just to relax.

You may argue that these tasks are not really what you want done but rather what *should* be done—they are for the benefit of your new child. Who will get up in the middle of the night to change the diaper? If your spouse doesn't do it, you will be forced to do it yourself—by default. You can't just let your baby spend the night crying.

> Why force responsibility of a task on the one who doesn't care if it's done?

But telling him what he should be doing is a poor motivator. It won't get the job done. Besides, to get your point across, you risk becoming very disrespectful—implying that your spouse is so out of touch that he doesn't even know or care what's best for your child.

While that may be precisely the way you feel, it's disrespectful. And I guarantee you that even if you're correct, your argument will be neither well received nor convincing. Whenever you try to impose your way of thinking on your spouse, you usually won't win. Instead, you'll simply drive your spouse away from you. So how can you do what needs to be done when you've run out of time to do it and your spouse is unwilling to help?

One possibility is to hire someone. It's a much better idea than working yourself to exhaustion or trying to force your spouse to do it. Hiring a housekeeper half a day each week to do only the most unpleasant cleaning chores is money well spent. The same thing can be said about maintaining the yard. Having someone mow and trim the lawn can turn a burdensome Saturday into an opportunity to enjoy the day with the family.

After you look at the remaining items on the original list more closely, you may decide to change your attitude about some of the tasks. When you know that the only way to get something done is

Try This

Try creating a cooking co-op with three other couples in your area who are willing to join. Assign one evening (Monday through Thursday) to each family. One night a week, you'll have to cook and deliver food to all the families, but you can turn this into a family project. And the other three nights, you'll have supper delivered to your door!

to hire someone, you may decide that it doesn't need to be done after all. In fact, you may find that what kept you convinced of its importance was the notion that your spouse was supposed to do it.

As Amy and Ed looked over their list of unassigned responsibilities, they may have assigned some of them as follows:

Unassigned Responsibilities	Solution
Cook and serve dinner on Friday and Saturday	Add Friday dinner to Ed's list; order pizza on Saturday nights
Mop kitchen and bathroom floors	Hire neighbor girl for one hour each week
Wipe down counters and fixtures in kitchen and bathroom	Add to Amy's list

Dual Careers Carry Added Expenses

The mistake that most dual-career couples make is to assume that the second income should be as free of additional expense as possible. What that means, of course, is that the second earner is expected to work all day and then do everything she would have done if it were not for her job. But those tasks can't be easily added to either the husband or wife's schedule if they are both working.

My solution of hiring help to ease the load is a hard sell for most couples. If some or even most of the income is lost, why work outside the home? Why pay for extra child care and household tasks when you could do them yourself if you didn't have a second career?

Keep in mind that there are many intangible benefits to dual careers. Compensation increases with years on the job, so spouses who work while raising their children will earn much more after the children have left the nest. So even if you only break even after paying someone else to fulfill domestic responsibilities, you're building your earning potential for the future. One of the most important reasons why women on average earn less than men is that they don't usually have the same years of experience in a particular career. By taking time from their jobs to raise their children, they suffer a financial disadvantage when they return to work.

Another benefit to dual careers is that there's something very energizing and uplifting about getting away from full-time domestic responsibilities. Even if the money earned doesn't quite cover the cost of replacement child care and housework, a full-time or even a part-time career is a welcome escape that many mothers need.

Of course, there are also benefits to being a full-time parent. Mothers who postpone their education or career to stay at home or even homeschool their children usually have very few regrets. Amy was leaning toward that choice, but it usually means less income at a time in life when financial pressures are greatest.

SOUND FAMILIAR?

Erica joined her three-year-old daughter, Kelli, and her husband, Jason, as they played together in the living room. Erica still had a dessert to bake for tomorrow's party, but she wanted to spend time with her family first since she hadn't seen them all day.

Two hours later, after putting Kelli to bed and ironing some laundry, Erica finally started her baking. Glancing at the clock, which read 9:30, she wished she'd just bought a cake at the grocery store. *But Jason would've been upset,* she thought. *We shouldn't be spending money on desserts I can bake myself.*

A compromise implemented by an increasing number of couples is developing home-based careers that allow both career and child care to exist side by side. This provides added income to pay for household help and baby-sitters, but still leaves time to care for your children. My daughter and daughter-in-law both have chosen this option with very satisfactory results. In fact, they both have homeschooled their children while maintaining their careers.

Most dual-career couples mistakenly assume that the second income should be as free of additional expense as possible.

His Work, Her Work

When you've finished step three of my plan to create a fair division of labor, you're left with two lists of household and child-care responsibilities—one for him and one for her. There should be nothing left on the original list. And all tasks should fit into your schedules so that no one is exhausted with the burden of too much work.

But what if one of you doesn't fulfill your responsibilities? What should you do if your spouse agrees to diaper your child every other evening but then ignores the task when it arises?

This problem may have more to do with unformed habits than the shirking of responsibility. If you really don't mind doing the tasks you've been assigned, you may still neglect doing them because they haven't yet become habits. But you can get into the routine of doing them easily enough by simple repetition.

For a few weeks, you may need to remind yourself that this task must be done every other day. Leave yourself a note on your schedule that the diaper must be checked every hour or so during the evening. If necessary, get a watch that buzzes every hour as an added reminder. After a few weeks of practice, you'll be thinking about diapers more than you've ever imagined!

Once you have a fair division of labor, you can move to the next step in my plan. This step will help you feel much better about my solution, and it will also help you deposit extra love units into each other's Love Bank.

Step 4: Assume or share some responsibilities that deposit the most love units.

Up to this point, the assignment of household responsibilities is fair. You're dividing responsibilities according to willingness and motivation. But marriage takes you one step further. In marriage, you do things for each other because you care about each other's feelings, not just because you want them done yourself. And that can make huge Love Bank deposits if done the right way.

You may not be willing to take responsibility of a certain task because, quite frankly, you don't think it needs to be done. But if your spouse thinks it needs to be done, helping out may make him or her incredibly happy.

To be sure your effort is not wasted, both you and your spouse should add one more piece of information to your list of responsibilities. Beside each task, write another number indicating how many love units you think would be deposited if your spouse would help you with that task or do it for you once in a while. Use a scale from 0 to 5, with 0 indicating that you would experience no pleasure and 5 indicating that you would experience maximum pleasure and would be eternally grateful.

This is a sample of some tasks from Ed and Amy's list:

Try This

Working parents and stay-at-home parents can complement each other. A stay-at-home mom might perform a few household tasks for a working mom, providing a small extra income for the stay-at-home mom (enough to cover baby-sitters while she and her husband spend time alone) while alleviating pressures on the working mom.

Amy's Responsibilities	Love Units Ranking	Ed's Responsibilities	Love Units Ranking
Bathe and dress Ryan M–Th	2	Bathe and dress Ryan on weekends	3
Dust living room and bedrooms	2	Vacuum living room and bedrooms	4
Cook and serve dinner M–Th	4	Cook and serve dinner on Sunday	2
Wipe down counters and fixtures in bathroom and kitchen	5	Cook and serve dinner on Friday evening	5

If these ratings are accurate, it means that whenever you have completed a task that was rated 4 or 5 by your spouse, you will be depositing lots of love units. Why not cook dinner or iron shirts or pick up socks if it helps preserve the feeling of love your spouse has for you? But don't waste your time and energy doing tasks of lesser importance to your spouse.

> Why not cook dinner or pick up socks if it preserves the feeling of love your spouse has for you?

Your spouse's response to your help should prove whether or not you're making Love Bank deposits. If your spouse thanks you when you perform the task and expresses his or her appreciation with affection, you know you are on the right track. But if your spouse ignores you after performing one of these tasks, love units are not being deposited for some reason. In that case go back to your spouse's original list of tasks and pick something else to do that has a greater impact.

Just because you decide to help your spouse with one of his or her household responsibilities doesn't make it your responsibility. In fact, if your spouse starts assuming that it's now your responsibility, you are unlikely to deposit as many love units when you do it. As soon as your spouse takes your care for granted, its effect will be diluted.

But if your spouse sees a burdensome task as his or her responsibility and you help with that task, he or she will appreciate the help you give. So the first three steps of my plan for a fair division of labor are crucial because they establish responsibility. Unless you first agree that a task is your spouse's responsibility, your efforts to help will tend to be taken for granted.

Another important reminder is that if you decide to help your spouse, be sure that it's something you enjoy doing. If you find the effort to be unpleasant, whatever love units you deposit into your spouse's account will be withdrawn from your account. So you must do these tasks for your spouse in ways that are not burdensome for you.

There may be no obvious way for you to enjoy doing an entire task for your spouse. After all, if you enjoyed doing it, you would have made it one of your responsibilities. But you might not mind helping your spouse with it or doing part of a task. For example, one of you might not mind making dinner if the other person were to clean up afterwards. Or you might enjoy helping your spouse clean up after dinner as long as you are to do it together.

> ### Try This
>
> Ask your children to help you surprise your spouse by completing some household tasks. They are usually more willing to help with chores if it's part of a special plan.

From Frantic to Fulfilled

Do you feel overwhelmed by domestic tasks? If so, it's time for a fair division of labor. And the solution to this problem is very logical: Figure out what needs to be done and then assign tasks to the one who enjoys doing it or wants it done the most. Once the assignments are made, make sure you both can fulfill these tasks after eight hours of sleep each night, fifteen hours of undivided attention each week, and fifteen hours of quality family time each week. Then, as a way of making extra Love Bank deposits, help each other out once in a while.

There's only one right way to divide household and child-care tasks, and that's to do it with mutual agreement. Quite frankly, it's the way all decisions should be made in marriage, because it's not only the wisest way, but it also protects your love for each other. This approach to the division of household responsibilities guarantees your mutual care, especially when you feel like being uncaring. And it prevents you from trying to force your spouse into an unpleasant way of life.

So don't spend any more frantic days trying to keep your house from falling apart. Put an end to disagreements about household chores and create a plan that works for both of you. With a fair division of labor in place, your marriage will be headed for happiness, fulfillment, and best of all, the feeling of love.

Parenting Takes Time
How to Be a Committed Mom and Dad

I come from a long line of productive ancestors. Rudolph and Mary Harley had their first child, Rudolph Harley II, while on their voyage to America in 1719. Rudolph II grew up to be the father of thirteen children. His eighth child, Henry, had sixteen. Harley families continued to flourish through the generations, and finally a man named John Harley came along. His fifth child was Willard—my dad.

Where would I be without large families?

And where would my grandchildren be? Both of my children married the fifth and youngest child in their families!

Yet when it came time for Joyce and me to raise a family, we stopped after having only two. We found that the second child turned out to be quite a handful when we added to it the ongoing demands of the first child. And sadly, I wasn't much help to Joyce when our second child arrived. I was still in graduate school and working full time to support our family. I assumed that I had enough to do—Joyce would

173

have to take full responsibility of the children as a stay-at-home mom. And I ignored the fact that she needed me to help her with our children.

I made the same mistake Ed made in the last chapter—I unilaterally decided that Joyce would provide most of the child care and housework. I thought it was fair at the time, but if Joyce and I had made a joint decision regarding our division of labor, I probably would have rearranged my priorities, perhaps taking a little more time to finish school.

> Failure to meet the need for family commitment has destroyed many marriages and handicapped many children.

But my mistake wasn't just a failure to create a fair division of labor. It was also a failure to meet a very important emotional need—the need for family commitment. By turning over care of our children to Joyce, I left her with the impression that I was not her partner in raising them.

Joyce's need for family commitment was something I hadn't anticipated. And it grew right along with our children. If I had it to do over again, Joyce and I would have created a fair division of labor, one that would have been decided mutually. But I would have gone one step further—I would have also taken greater responsibility for the training of our children during those early years.

How about your marriage? Are you both involved in child training, or does the responsibility fall on one spouse? If you'd like to make the most of your time as a parent while also meeting your spouse's need for family commitment, read on.

"He Shows Such Little Interest in His Child . . ."

Failure to meet the need for family commitment has destroyed many marriages—and handicapped many children. Bonnie could see her marriage fading fast, so she wrote to me for advice when her husband seemed to lose all interest in his second child.

Dear Dr. Harley,

I gave birth to a beautiful and healthy baby girl last month. We already have a three-year-old son, John. My husband, Keith, was very excited while I was pregnant with John and pitched in every once in a while when John was an infant. Even now that he's three, Keith usually spends a few hours on Sundays with him.

However, Keith has shown almost no interest in our daughter, Rachel. He never could get "up" during the pregnancy and barely has any time for her now that she's with us (he didn't even want to be in the delivery room, as he was for our son).

This is causing a lot of stress in our relationship. I can't deal with the fact that he has such little interest in his new child. This lack of interest has also been transferred to me. My priorities right now are my children, especially my daughter, who needs all of me, but my husband's lack of support is driving me crazy. It's gotten so bad that I'm considering moving in with my parents for a while. At least they'll be willing to help out. I've tried talking to him about it, but as far as he's concerned, raising children is a woman's job. I'm at a loss. HELP!

Bonnie

There were at least two factors causing trouble in Bonnie and Keith's marriage. The first was Keith's lack of interest in child care, particularly as it applied to Rachel. The second was Bonnie's lack of interest in Keith, since she was so consumed in caring for their new daughter. Either of these factors alone could have ruined their marriage. But the combination of the two was having devastating consequences.

Failure to Be a Father

As I mentioned earlier, the feeling of love is essential for a happy marriage, but it's very fragile. Most couples lose it within a few years, especially after children arrive.

Sometimes love dies simply because spouses are lazy about the way they try to meet each other's needs. But more often, it's not laziness that gets them in trouble—it's ignorance. Spouses are unaware of the time it takes to meet each other's intimate emotional needs, and they feel that earning more money or caring for the children is more important than scheduling that time together.

> The need for family commitment has little to do with a fair division of labor—it's about being partners in the development of children.

However, they can also be ignorant of something else—new emotional needs that are created very unexpectedly.

If our emotional needs stayed the same before and after marriage, the problem of meeting them would be easy to fix—just go back to what we did before marriage. And some emotional needs do stay consistent enough throughout life that we can do just that. Intimate affection and conversation, sexual fulfillment, and recreational companionship are needs that spouses should keep meeting for each other. But there are new emotional needs that can develop after marriage, especially when children arrive.

One of these new emotional needs—family commitment—can come as a big surprise to spouses, particularly men. If you're happy and fulfilled when your spouse puts time and energy into child care and training, and frustrated when little or no interest is shown, you have this need.

The need for family commitment has little to do with a fair division of labor. Instead, it's about being partners in the development of children. Bonnie was not complaining about Keith's lack of help, she was concerned about his lack of interest in his new daughter.

While family commitment can be an emotional need for some men, it's almost universal for women. Bonnie definitely had this need, and Keith was failing to meet it. Using my terminology, every time Keith took time to be with his children and contribute to their care, he deposited love units into Bonnie's Love Bank because he was meeting one of her important emotional needs. But when he ignored his children, he withdrew love units and left her frustrated and unfulfilled. His failure to care for his children was putting the future of their relationship at risk.

Failure to Be a Wife

Bonnie made it clear in her letter that Keith was failing to meet her need for family commitment. But Bonnie was also failing to meet Keith's emotional needs. She wrote, "My priorities right now are my children, especially my daughter, who needs all of me." That meant she was not making very many Love Bank deposits into Keith's account. And her neglect was leading to sizable withdrawals.

When a husband and wife stop meeting each other's important emotional needs, a negative feedback loop is created. Suppose that you and your spouse sleep with a dual-control electric blanket. You like it cool, and your spouse likes it warm. Then one night your controls are accidentally switched. What happens? You find your side of the bed too warm, so you turn your control down. Your spouse then finds his or her side of the bed too cool and turns the control up. As you get hotter and finally turn off your control completely, your spouse gets colder and turns his or her control all the way up. Your bed eventually becomes unbearable for both of you.

That's what can happen when emotional needs aren't met. If you fail to meet your spouse's emotional needs from time to time, your spouse becomes less motivated to meet yours as often as you would like. As your spouse loses interest in meeting your needs, you become even less motivated to meet his or her needs. And eventually, neither of you is meeting the other's needs at all.

That's what probably happened to Bonnie and Keith. When Keith failed to meet Bonnie's emotional need for family commitment, she became less motivated to meet his intimate emotional needs. He may have been confused about why he was receiving the cold shoulder and then justified his behavior by assuming that raising children was "a woman's job"—that he was doing his part by earning a living to support them. He may have thought that what she was asking of him went way beyond the call of duty. And as he became increasingly unwilling to help her with the children, she became increasingly unwilling to meet his intimate emotional needs.

Who Started It?

I've been assuming that Keith's lack of interest in Bonnie's second pregnancy may have triggered her reluctance to meet his intimate emotional needs. But it's just as likely that she became so focused on caring for her first child that she failed to meet his needs before their second child arrived.

Maybe he'd been doing a good job meeting her need for family commitment. He seemed to show much more interest in her pregnancy with John and was still involved with him, at least on Sunday afternoons. Yet when Bonnie became a mother, she may have stopped being Keith's lover—not exactly what he had in mind when he married her.

Keith's frustration at the failure of having his intimate emotional needs met may have drained her account in his Love Bank. And by the time of her second pregnancy, he may have lost his love for her entirely. That loss of love would have left him with less motivation to attend to her needs during pregnancy and to care for their new daughter. His neglect would have emptied his account in her Love Bank, leading her to consider a separation—if not outright divorce.

If it *was* Bonnie's rearrangement of priorities—making her children's happiness a higher priority than Keith's happiness—then that decision was certainly misguided. It's a couple's love for each other that guarantees the most happiness for their children, and that's threatened when anything else becomes a higher priority.

It's anybody's guess who started the negative feedback loop. But regardless of who started it, eventually they were probably both contributing to it. While the future of their marriage seems bleak, there is a solution to Bonnie and Keith's problem. If they implement it soon, their marriage and the happiness of their children will be secure.

What's the Solution?

The only way couples can break the negative feedback loop of unmet needs is for them to start meeting each other's emotional needs, in spite of their poor motivation to do so. I know that's easier said than done, but it's the solution.

A coach makes people do what they don't feel like doing so they can have what they want. And that's what my job as a marriage counselor often requires, at least in the beginning. Most couples I counsel don't want to meet each other's emotional needs, because their own needs haven't been met. They want their emotional needs met first. But I explain to them that they'll both have to meet each other's emotional needs at the same time, even if they don't feel like doing it right away.

Think about the electric blanket analogy, in which each person controlled the blanket temperature of the other. In this same way, neither person in a marriage can meet his or her own emotional needs. Intimate affection, intimate conversation, sexual fulfillment, recreational companionship, and family commitment are all something *someone else* must do to make them happy.

Bonnie's need for family commitment affects her in two ways. First, she wants a greater degree of participation from Keith—she wants him to be involved with her in the care and training of her children. But second, she feels that her involvement with her children prevents her from meeting his needs the way she has in the past. This instinct to take her attention away from Keith and redirect it at her children leads to marital disaster. It not only makes it less likely for Keith to be an active participant in the training of their children, it also makes it more likely that they'll eventually get divorced.

When someone fails to meet their spouse's needs, it's less likely that their own needs will be met.

If Bonnie were to override her maternal instinct to give her children most of her attention, and keep caring for Keith as she had before their arrival, he would be more motivated to become the father his children need. And if he fulfilled that duty, he would meet her need for family commitment.

Keith was off to a good start when John was born. He was concerned for Bonnie's health while she was pregnant, and he took an active interest in caring for John after he arrived. But something had changed by the time Rachel was born, and my best guess is that their romantic relationship had ended. With its demise, they probably also lost their love for each other.

So my plan to restore their marriage had to accomplish two objectives. They should restore their romantic relationship by taking fifteen hours every week to meet each other's intimate emotional needs, and Keith should commit another fifteen hours for quality family time. That way, he could get back to where he was when John was born—in love with Bonnie and an enthusiastic father to their children.

So what about this need for family commitment? How could Keith fill it—and how can you fill it along with all of the other responsibilities of your own marriage? Are we running out of time for the average couple? Is all of this becoming unrealistic?

Making Quality Family Time Happen

Throughout this chapter, I'll frequently refer to a husband as the one who needs to meet his wife's need for family commitment. But it's important to note that husbands can also have this need, so wives should also meet it. Quite frankly, whether or not you have this need, your children's future depends on your commitment to train them properly. So I suggest you do what it takes to meet this need, even if you aren't sure either of you has it.

What happens when you don't schedule time to achieve a goal? Usually, other less important goals will crowd it out. And unless you put it into your schedule, that goal sits on the back burner.

> Quality family time is not child care—it's a time for child training.

I've already stressed the importance of scheduling time each week for undivided attention to achieve the goal of meeting each other's intimate emotional needs. But the same must also be done if you want to meet the need for family commitment—you must schedule time for it. But how much time should you schedule, and what should you do with that time?

My experience counseling hundreds of wives who have expressed a need for family commitment has given me answers to those questions. It takes about the same number of hours to meet this one need as it takes to meet the four intimate emotional needs—about fifteen hours a week of quality family time. The reason that it can't be done in less time is that child training requires an emotional bonding between parents and children. And I've found that about fifteen hours of quality contact usually does the job.

Technically, the need for family commitment is not met simply by spending time with your children—it's met by using that time to train them to become successful adults. Spending *quality* family time together lets kids know that their parents love them and want them to be happy.

But some children need more training than others. If your children are struggling emotionally, or if you are having discipline problems with them, more than fifteen hours a week is recommended, at least on a temporary basis. By adding training time with your children, you can better understand the problems they are facing and the effectiveness of your plans to help them overcome those problems.

I've already mentioned that quality family time is not child care—it's a time when the entire family is together for the purpose of teaching life values. And it's ideal to have the family together as a unit during this time, because thoughtfulness and mutual care, among the most important life values, are best taught with the opportunity to practice on others within the family.

Your time together should be enjoyable; it shouldn't be spent lecturing your children. That would make it unpleasant for everyone. Instead, it should be spent practicing mutual care with games or fun activities until it becomes a habit.

For instance, while you're having meals together, you can focus on good table manners, listening when someone is talking instead of interrupting, and learning to say please and thank you when food is passed. In this way, you can teach your children that table etiquette rules are a way of being sensitive to the feelings of others.

The same can be done when taking a walk as a family, playing games together, attending sporting events, and working on family projects. The example you both set as parents, showing care toward each other and your children, goes a long way toward demonstrating how they are to behave to others.

In fact, almost all behavior we consider "good" and "bad" revolves around the issue of thoughtfulness. So it's a wise idea to use quality family time as an opportunity to teach this important trait. The sooner children learn how to be thoughtful, the easier they are to raise and the more successful they'll become as adults.

> The sooner children learn how to be thoughtful, the easier they are to raise, and the more successful they'll become as adults.

If your primary theme is the consideration of people's feelings, common parenting problems are easier to address. Fighting, which is instinctive in most children, can be nipped in the bud because children will be taught that fighting is a failure to care. Picking up toys, cleaning up a room, and toning down playful running and screaming are all instances of thoughtfulness. By focusing a child's attention on the feelings of others early in life, the child will grow up to become a considerate adult.

Of course, thoughtfulness doesn't mean that children must sacrifice their own happiness to make others happy. It means that as they do what makes them happy, they make others happy too. In other words, they don't gain at the expense of others. Sounds familiar, doesn't it?

Since discipline is an essential part of child training, I suggest the following guidelines to help make your discipline effective. They will help you put quality into Quality Family Time.

Explain the Rules

Parents often teach their children that being obedient is good and being disobedient is bad. And you'll get away with that argument for the first few years, because very young children don't understand complex concepts such as thoughtfulness. All they understand is that if they obey, they'll be rewarded, and if they disobey, they'll be punished.

For example, if you want your young child to stop knocking your table lamp to the ground, slapping his or her hand can be very effective. Without a mild form of corporal punishment, small children will run wild and destroy half of what you own. At that age all they understand is that obedience is good and disobedience is bad.

But it doesn't take long before explanations not only are understood but are demanded by children. "Why?" is a question that young inquisitive minds seem to ask instinctively. And that's the best time to have an answer.

"Why should I clean up my room?"

"Why should I sit at the table after my dinner is done?"

"Why should I stop throwing my ball across the room?"

If your answer to those questions is "Because I told you so," you are laying an ethical foundation that might makes right. Whoever is bigger and stronger gets to have his or her way. If that's how they interpret your rules, they'll be biding their time until they're away from your control and can do what they please. And then they can impose their will on others who are weaker.

While it's tempting to make rules to help you survive the parenting years, unless those rules have a deeper and more ethical meaning, your children will eventually interpret them as good for you and bad for them. Instead, your rules should clearly show that you have your children's best interest in mind, even when your kids are very young. They should have profound meaning and logic, even if they aren't yet completely understood.

As your children grow, they'll eventually come to understand that your rules make sense. And quality family time is a great time to explain the rationale for rules. But you must follow those same principles of mutual caring yourself. That way, your children will continue to follow them long after they have children of their own.

SOUND FAMILIAR?

Looking for an evening snack, Ben walked into the kitchen, where his daughter, Casey, was finishing up her homework. Noticing the dishes stacked up in the sink from dinner, he told Casey to wash them up.

Casey started to protest, "But Dad, I helped cook dinner and clear the table. And I have homework to do. Why should I have to do the dishes too?"

Ben grabbed a bag of chips from the cupboard and replied, "Because I told you so. And your whining won't change my mind."

Quite frankly, when you behave in ways that violate the principles you are trying to teach, it not only sets a bad example, it also indicates that you don't take your role seriously. When you are thoughtless, you should apologize and let your children know thoughtfulness is a lifelong effort.

> Unless your rules have a deeper meaning, your children will interpret them as good for you and bad for them.

Be Consistent

If you're not careful, you as a parent can turn into a dictator. When power goes to people's heads, they end up hurting the ones they're supposed to protect. And it happens because they don't have anyone putting pressure on them to be consistent in the way they carry out their mission.

When your children are small, you should demand obedience, because children don't know what's good for them—you must punish behavior that's destructive and reward behavior that's constructive. But most parents don't know how to stick to the overarching ground rules of care for their children as they grow. What begins as a demand for obedience that's in the child's best interest can become a demand for obedience that's only in the interest of the parent. And the older children become, the more they resent this kind of treatment.

Your children should feel confident that the rules you create are in their best interest. And even though the rules themselves and the way they are applied may change over time, the overriding principle of your care shouldn't change. When your children are old enough to understand the rules, it should be clear to them that you've been consistent in doing what's in their best interest all along.

Consistency also means that you don't change the rules as your mood changes. Parents often make the mistake of being overly generous to their children when they're happy and hardhearted when they're unhappy. One day their children are running wild and the next day they're locked up in their rooms—all because of a change in mood.

> Consistency means that you don't change the rules as your mood changes.

But when parents follow the Policy of Joint Agreement in meting out rewards and discipline, it helps smooth out inconsistencies, because both parents are rarely in a generous or hardhearted mood at the same time. Your children want a consistently caring mom and dad, not an unpredictable dictator. So follow the rules independently of the mood you happen to be in, and your children will be much better behaved.

Discipline Appropriately

As I mentioned earlier, appropriate discipline changes with age. Children under six months should not be disciplined at all, because they aren't able to understand cause and effect. By the time they reach one year of age, they should be punished for specific behavior, such

SOUND FAMILIAR?

Marita sighed as she heard raised voices coming from the basement. Knowing that rainy weather was keeping her three sons cooped up in the house, she'd let them play outdoor games in the basement for the last few days. But tonight, with a headache throbbing behind her eyes, she was in no mood to put up with it.

"Kids," she yelled, "you know you're not supposed to play with the football inside. Now knock it off and go sit in your rooms for the next half hour."

"But Mom," her oldest boy responded, "you let us play football inside yesterday. Why are we being punished now? It's not fair!"

as touching electric plug sockets, and rewarded for specific behavior, such as in toilet training.

Corporal punishment is usually appropriate for children under eight years old, as long as it's on their bottoms and never leaves a mark. But after eight, punishment should focus on the suspension of privileges.

By age eleven, the principle behind every rule should be clearly explained and understood, because that's when children have the ability to understand higher principles of mutual care and concern. And it's at that time that parents should implement a plan of slowly letting go, giving their children increased freedom to make their own decisions and take responsibility for the outcome.

There's never a good time for a divorce from a child's perspective. But the worst time is at the beginning of puberty (ages eleven through thirteen). It's in these years that children set standards that will follow them throughout life. Divorce teaches them some very bad lessons—that parents don't care about each other and don't care about them. And from a child's perspective, divorce teaches the lesson that self-centered independence is far more appropriate than caring relationships because relationships can't be trusted. All the training you have given your children to be thoughtful goes down the drain when you divorce. That's one of the main reasons why children of divorced parents tend to be thoughtless.

> There's never a good time for a divorce from a child's perspective.

By the age of sixteen, most children are beyond child training. Their parents have a few more years to feed, clothe, and house them, but the training days are over. Parents who try to control misbehavior or disrespect with punishment find that it can backfire in a most tragic way. I've counseled scores of teenagers who have run away from home or even attempted suicide as a reaction to something as benign as being grounded. And even rewards for good behavior don't have the same positive effect they would have had in the past.

I'm not saying that children can't learn at that age. In fact, children learn better than ever in their late teen years. It's just that what is commonly regarded as child training is not as effective. Instead, these teenagers want to be treated as adults by their parents. Respectful discussion is always appropriate, and teens can learn from these discussions, but parents should expect quite a bit of independent thinking. And they shouldn't expect their children to be quite as respectful of them as they should be of their children.

I can remember long conversations I had with my father when I was a teenager. I doubted almost everything he believed in and challenged him at every turn. But he was respectful in the way we discussed these issues, and I remember many of his answers even today. While he was respectful of my doubts, I don't think I was as respectful of his beliefs. But because of his respect, he had a great influence on my way of thinking, although at the time I'm sure he didn't know it. I rarely let on when he said something that impressed me.

It's a point I make repeatedly—if you want to influence others, you must begin with respect for their perspective.

Reach Agreements Together

I've already mentioned that child training should be a joint effort between spouses, but it bears repeating. Whether it's regarding a punishment or a reward, parents should first reach agreement. When parents are united in their child-training efforts, their words and actions carry more weight, creating greater respect in their children. And when your children know that you're in agreement, they're far less likely to challenge your decision.

Meeting the need for family commitment requires that husbands treat parenting as a joint responsibility with their wives. Wives don't want to be left with all the child care and then have their husbands sweep in with decisions about values and discipline. All decisions regarding the values to be taught and methods used to teach them should be made with mutual enthusiastic agreement.

The Four Guidelines for Successful Negotiation should be implemented whenever you and your spouse have a conflict over discipline. It may seem awkward and time-consuming when you're first introduced to these guidelines, but with practice, you can zip right through all four in a matter of minutes when a child needs discipline. And the telephone can help you make these decisions on the spot, instead of waiting hours after the problem first surfaced.

> Wives don't want to be left with all the child care and then have their husbands sweep in with decisions about values and discipline.

If you want to meet the need for family commitment, you and your spouse must work together as a team to direct your children toward good behavior.

Control Anger

Some people feel that anger is a good way to communicate displeasure. It certainly gets the attention of children, and it also tends to

SOUND FAMILIAR?

It had been a long day for Cynthia. Her seven-year-old son, Sam, had been tired and cranky all day, bossing his little sister around and talking back when he was reprimanded. As punishment for his poor behavior, Cynthia told him he couldn't watch any television all day.

When her husband, Brian, returned home from work, Sam didn't waste any time trying to subvert his mom. In an innocent voice he asked, "Dad, can I watch a video while Mom finishes making supper?" Cynthia cringed as Brian replied, "Sure, buddy."

make them obey, at least in the short term. But no child psychologist I've ever studied recommends anger as a tool for training children.

There's a host of reasons why experts advise parents to keep anger under control. Anger doesn't teach the lessons of mutual respect and care. In fact, it teaches exactly the opposite—that if you are threatening, you can get what you want. And besides, whatever it is you teach with anger will not be learned. All your children will learn is to get out of your way, and once they're on their own, they'll remember you as an abusive parent.

> Whatever you try to teach with anger will not be learned.

So control your anger before you discipline your children. By separating your emotions from the disciplinary action, you'll become a much more effective parent. And instead of withdrawing love units from your account in your spouse's Love Bank, your method of discipline will deposit them.

Quality Family Time Pays Off

Setting aside quality family time each week may seem like a tall order. And many parents don't think it's worth trying. As I said earlier, it's tempting to simply act like a dictator to your kids—taking the easy path of demands, disrespect, and anger.

But good parenting *does* require time and commitment. And in the end, it's a lot easier than bad parenting—thoughtful children are much simpler to raise than thoughtless children.

In Keith and Bonnie's situation, Keith would have made it much easier for Bonnie to meet his intimate emotional needs if he'd continued to do what he had started when his son was born. Granted, Bonnie made a huge mistake by forgetting how to be a lover after John's arrival. But it would have been easier to persuade her to return to a romantic relationship if Keith had been a good father.

Besides, Keith wanted his children to grow up to be happy and successful adults just as much as Bonnie did. And parents who spend quality time with their children have a decisive influence on them.

Do you want to leave your child's training to their peers? Or would you rather take personal responsibility for their moral and educational development? Spending quality family time with your children is one of the most important things you'll ever do in life—it meets your spouse's need for family commitment and also guarantees your children a successful future.

> Spending quality family time with your children is one of the most important things you'll ever do in life.

Either of these reasons is enough to warrant quality family time. But when you put the two together, it's hard to imagine why anyone would ignore them. So next time you're tempted to dodge family commitment, just think about what's at stake—the health of your marriage and your children.

PART *3*

SPECIAL CASES

Mixed Families, Blended Lives
From Discord to Harmony

My wife, Joyce, wasn't sure she'd be a good mother. She hated to baby-sit when she was a teenager. The few children she did watch over usually irritated her, and she thought that her own children might have the same effect. But when Jennifer and Steven came along, she turned out to be a terrific mother. Caring for her children was entirely different from caring for someone else's children.

That's why things get so complicated when couples who already have kids marry. It's tough enough to raise your own children, but your spouse's children can make the task seem impossible. Mixed families face some very complex issues. And stepparents and stepchildren often end up resenting each other. That's one of the reasons why mixing families in second (or third) marriages is one of the greatest causes of divorce. Very few of these marriages survive, especially when divorce, rather than a spouse's death, puts an end to the nuclear family.

But if you find yourself in a mixed family, the situation isn't hopeless. There's a way to beat the odds, and I've seen many couples learn to create a wonderful, love-filled marriage. So what's the secret?

A Simple Rule

As I've mentioned many times already, the Policy of Joint Agreement is a simple rule to help spouses consider each other's feelings when they're tempted to be thoughtless. And in mixed families, this policy is the secret for parenting success. If you and your spouse get an early start on this rule and develop the habit of making mutually agreeable child-training decisions, the way you help raise each other's children will become comfortable for both of you—and for the children.

But if you get a late start and have already created child-training habits that benefit only one of you, the idea of following the Policy of Joint Agreement can seem daunting. When you first use it, you'll see that most of what you've been doing is thoughtless. You must change almost all of your child-training habits, and then you must still overcome all the resentment that's been built up from thoughtless decisions you've already made. So it makes sense to start a mixed marriage with the Policy of Joint Agreement.

> If you find yourself in a mixed family, the situation isn't hopeless. There's a way to beat the odds.

That's not how mixed marriages usually begin, however. They usually begin without mutual agreement when it comes to child training. Couples often feel guilty about their divorce and remarriage and want to make it up to their children by providing a particularly enjoyable lifestyle. What that usually means is very lax discipline and very spoiled children. And these couples also tend to give so much attention to their children that they fail to give their spouse the attention needed to stay in love.

In this chapter, you'll read three letters I've received from couples struggling with a mixed family. They're good illustrations of some typical problems faced by parents trying to raise each other's children. In each case, their problems arise from two failures: (1) failure to train children with mutual agreement and (2) failure to meet each other's intimate emotional needs. By overcoming failures in these two crucial areas, couples in mixed families can provide a healthy environment for their children and enjoy a fulfilling marriage.

To avoid any confusion, I define a **mixed** (sometimes called "blended") family or marriage as one in which at least one spouse has a child from another relationship. In a **nuclear** family or marriage, all the children are the offspring of both spouses.

"My Husband's Children Run Wild . . ."

The first letter is typical of hundreds I've received describing a very common problem in mixed families—a spouse uses one standard for his or her own children and another for the stepchildren. In this case, it was the husband who was using two different standards, but I've received just as many letters from husbands who complain that their wives' children are treated with special favors. In either case, this practice causes serious problems for a couple.

Dear Dr. Harley,

This is our second marriage for each of us. We each have two children, all of whom are older teens except one. We seem to constantly disagree on simple child-rearing issues (i.e. cleaning the room, household chores, curfew, etc.). My largest complaint is that since we have blended our families, it seems my children have had to make the most adjustments while my husband's children just seem to run wild when they are here (they live with their mother most of the time). My husband, George, is always very critical of my children and their failure to conform to house rules, yet his kids seem to make

their own rules. While his children are never punished, he continues
to punish mine for seemingly minor infractions. This is causing a
great deal of distrust among all of us. Is there anything we can do to
rebuild trust between us? I am beginning to question my faithfulness
to someone so unwilling to compromise.

Abby

Each spouse in a mixed family tends to put his or her own children's
interests first. It's usually in an effort to compensate for the trauma
their kids experienced at the death of a parent or divorce. The guilt
parents feel, having deprived their children of the advantages of a
nuclear family, often causes them to give the kids whatever they want.
Discipline goes down the drain and, as Abby has noted, they "just
seem to run wild."

How do you train children who have suffered through a tragedy?
They've already had enough sadness, parents reason. *Why should we
compound the problem by making them clean their room?*

And when the breakup of a family is due to divorce rather than
death, there's a special problem—the parents have set a very bad example. Instead
of teaching children how to be considerate of others, one or both parents have
proven to be so thoughtless that their love
was destroyed. When you add a failure
to discipline children to the bad example
that was set, you find yourself living with
savages.

> If you add a failure to discipline children to a bad example set by parents, you find yourself living with savages.

In Abby's case, George's children only
lived with them occasionally. But if they had lived there permanently,
she probably would have left him already. One of the reasons for
divorce in mixed families is that the bad behavior of stepchildren
simply drives their stepparents crazy.

But Abby has another common problem. While George may feel
overly protective of his own children out of guilt, he feels no such

guilt toward her children. So he disciplines them regularly to protect himself from their thoughtless behavior.

Abby wants fairness. She says that she wants George to treat his children the way he is treating her children. But she actually wants much more than that. Even if he were to treat all of them the same way, she would cringe whenever he was critical and harsh toward her children, because she feels the same protection and guilt toward them as he does toward his children. She's uncomfortable whenever her children are disciplined, regardless of who does the training. Yet she really doesn't want them running wild, either.

Love or Discipline?

Children raised by a divorced or unwed mother tend to get into more trouble than children raised in a nuclear family. And there's good reason why that's true.

A father and mother in a nuclear family usually bring two important child-training factors together—love and discipline. The mother is usually more loving and caring toward her children, while the father is more of a disciplinarian. The children know that the father loves them and that the mother won't let them get away with just anything. But in general, they tend to see their father as the enforcer and their mother as the caregiver.

Divorce, however, changes that delicate balance. A single parent must choose which of the two—love or discipline—will be emphasized. And mothers tend to choose love, while fathers tend to choose discipline. As a result, children raised by single mothers tend to be more unruly, while children raised by single fathers tend to feel less loved.

> Divorce changes the delicate balance between a mom's love and a dad's discipline.

Single parents usually think that remarriage will help the situation—the stepfather can provide rule enforcement to *her* children while the stepmother makes *his* children feel more loved. But the opposite often takes place. As Abby has discovered, children in mixed families can be less disciplined and also feel less loved than those raised by a single parent. Mixing a family can create the worst of both worlds.

George doesn't want to discipline his children because he wants them to know that he loves them. But he has no problem disciplining Abby's children because he thinks that's his role in their marriage—to be the disciplinarian.

Her children, however, probably feel that she no longer loves them because she allows him to punish them. They're probably learning very little about cleaning their rooms, household chores, and curfews because they're getting mixed messages. And they are most certainly feeling resentment that their mother placed them in an unsafe environment.

You Can Have Both

Both Abby and George want their own children to know they are loved, so they're reluctant to punish them. And I agree with that approach to raising children of divorced parents because punishment of any kind is usually upsetting to both child and parent. If a choice *must* be made between children feeling loved or children cleaning up their rooms, love trumps rules.

But there's a way for Abby and George to have love *and* discipline if they follow my advice. The secret to making children feel loved while also obeying the rules is found by following the Policy of Joint Agreement and scheduling quality family time.

If you recall, quality family time is when the entire family is together for the purpose of teaching children cooperation and care for each other. This time is essentially recreational, but the activities are planned with thoughtfulness in mind. It's time set aside to teach your children values you feel are most important. And that's decided with the Policy of Joint Agreement.

> There's a way for mixed families to have love *and* discipline if they follow my advice.

If parents want their children to be relatively well behaved and also feel that they are loved, they must agree enthusiastically about their child-training goals and methods. And they must also focus their attention on thoughtfulness when they spend time together as a family. This is true of parents in nuclear families as well as step-parents in mixed families.

But it's particularly difficult to implement these concepts in mixed families, because parents usually feel that they should have the right to make unilateral decisions when raising their own offspring. This leads to the problems faced by George and Abby—one set of rules and discipline methods for his children and another set for her children. It's not surprising that she feels he's being unfair.

With the Policy of Joint Agreement, they could develop household rules that would be consistent for both sets of children. Whether it's cleaning the room, household chores, or curfew, all of the children would be expected to behave in the same way—at least once they had reached a certain age. And if anyone were to "run wild," there would be a consequence applied regardless of the child. Abby would no longer complain that her children had to make the most adjustments.

But that's not the way they currently live. George is probably setting house rules to suit himself. And since her children probably annoy him more than his own children do, he holds them to a stricter standard. When his children come in late, it doesn't bother him—they were just having normal teenage fun. But when her children break curfew, the roof caves in.

It's also possible that he wants his children to enjoy being with him more than they enjoy being with their mother. Competition for the affection of children is very common among divorced parents. So whenever the kids visit, George wants to avoid anything—like punishment—that makes their time with him unpleasant.

It's likely that his overarching rule is "he who rules, makes the rules." But instead of teaching both his children and Abby's children the important human value of thoughtfulness, he's teaching them that "might makes right." His mood determines what children are expected to do. And as the one in the home with the most control, he's able to give greater benefits to his own kids than his wife's kids.

That's a terrible way to train children, of course, because they come to the conclusion that they can treat others the same way—when they have power, they can use it to their advantage and to everyone else's disadvantage. And that's the mentality of a bully. Theft, assault, rape, and almost all other crimes can be justified by values that give the strong the right to dominate the weak. And parents teach those terrible values when they raise children George's way.

The Policy of Joint Agreement would change all of that, because it gives both spouses *equal* control. If George and Abby were to follow this policy, neither would have the right to give a child anything unilaterally. Control would be shared, and that would change the values being taught. Instead of learning that the strong get whatever they want, children would learn that strength can build relationships when it's used to help others. As they watched their parent and stepparent share their strengths with each other, the children would understand the value of thoughtfulness.

> The Policy of Joint Agreement gives both spouses *equal* control.

George may not want to punish his children when they come over, and that's okay. But he should not punish her children either, unless she is in enthusiastic agreement. And if he wants to set rules for her children, it's unlikely that she'll agree to them if they don't apply to his children as well.

If the threat of punishment were minimized in the way they train both sets of children, and if the value of thoughtfulness were emphasized to both sets of children during quality family time, Abby would be greatly relieved. Her children would not necessarily be perfect, but she and George would have a powerful influence on them because they'd be in agreement. Household rules would be described as examples of thoughtfulness, and they both would set a good example of thoughtfulness by following the Policy of Joint Agreement.

In the end, both sets of children would be better off if their parent and stepparent were united in child training. They would feel loved when their parents spent quality time with them. And they'd become better behaved as fair punishments and rewards were applied to them all.

When Life Becomes Unbearable

The following letter is another illustration of a wife's frustration when her husband treats his children with more leniency than he treats her children. But this case is worse than the one we've just seen—Betty's husband has full custody of his children.

Dear Dr. Harley,

Henry and I have been married two years, second marriage for both of us. I have two children, twelve and fourteen, and he has two, nineteen and seventeen. We both have full custody of our children. My kids are really good, but my husband is unforgiving when they forget to shut off a light or fail to do one of their chores. His children on the other hand have been in trouble with the law, were involved in teenage pregnancies, and more. But their behavior seems to be irrelevant. I am constantly on the defensive because he refuses to see the good side of my children. He is always right there to point out what they do wrong. Any suggestions on how I can break down this barrier? Our marriage was great at first, but it has become intolerable. Thanks so much!

Betty

In the last case we discussed, Abby had to endure her stepchildren occasionally. But poor Betty lives with them day in and day out. In both cases, their husbands made the mistake of applying a higher standard of discipline to their stepchildren than they did to their own children. And when their wives expressed resentment about such unfair behavior, the men ignored those reactions, leaving the wives to wonder, "Did he marry me just to have someone help raise his children?"

My solution for Betty is the same as my solution for Abby—follow the Policy of Joint Agreement and spend quality family time every week with the children. But there's one additional point that needs to be made.

Suppose that Henry were to accept all of the advice I gave George. He would follow the Policy of Joint Agreement regarding rules and discipline. He would overcome his unforgiving reaction to Betty's children when lights were left on and chores were left incomplete. He would also become more encouraging and admiring of her children. Would that fix Betty's problem?

Not necessarily. There are some marriages in which children are so undisciplined that a stepparent simply can't endure their thoughtlessness and their parent simply can't control their behavior. In spite of Henry's best efforts, his children could still run Betty out of the house.

> There are some marriages in which children are so undisciplined that a stepparent simply can't endure their thoughtlessness and their parent simply can't control their behavior.

Children of divorced parents tend to get into more trouble in their teen years than children who are raised in a nuclear family. So it's no surprise that Henry's children are behaving badly. What's surprising is that Betty's children are doing so well! Some of the differences might be attributed to their ages—Henry's children are nineteen and seventeen, while Betty's are only twelve and fourteen. But Betty still deserves credit for raising well-behaved children—children that age can be terrors.

Consider the case of Anthony and Penny. When they married, his thirteen-year-old-daughter, Mary, was not pleased. She resented Penny living with them and wanted her dad all to herself. Penny tried to be a caring stepmom, but competition between her and Mary escalated by the week. Mary became increasingly abusive toward Penny, and Anthony couldn't seem to stop it.

It all came to a head when Penny came home one day to find her clothes cut up into pieces. Mary had taken scissors and ruined what she thought was a woman's most precious possession—her clothes. My recommendation was for Penny to move out. There was no telling what Mary would do next.

I have witnessed many cases like Anthony and Penny's, in which the children of one spouse have upset the other spouse so much that they simply couldn't live together. When that's been the case, I've recommended a separation until the children have completed high school and are on their own or until the parents are able to protect each other from their children's bad behavior. But it's a very special separation.

In the separation I recommend, a husband and wife spend part of every day together—without the children. And during that time they meet each other's intimate emotional needs. If their children have caused them to lose their love for each other, the separation actually helps bring them back together again emotionally, restoring their love. And when they have not yet lost their love for each other, the separation helps keep it that way.

I've seen several dozen couples of mixed marriages who have separated because they could not protect each other from their children's bad behavior. In almost every case, they were eventually reunited. Some reunited after a very short separation, because the children themselves decided to accept the stepparent. For others, the couple had to wait until the children were on their own.

Did you notice that I suggested high school graduation as the moment of departure? It's an age when I believe most children become adult enough to be on their own. If they want to continue their education, grants and loans that pay for tuition as well as living expenses are readily available. Education can be particularly affordable if vocational, community, or state colleges are chosen. Or if they choose to go right to work from high school, they can live on their own by sharing living expenses with roommates.

Living at home after age eighteen can give kids a very unrealistic view of the value of money. Instead of learning to budget wisely, using their income as a guide of what they can afford to buy, they don't take into account the benefits that parents continue to provide. If you are to be poor at one time in your life, it should be when you are young.

> When the situation becomes unbearable for one spouse, they risk losing all their love for their husband or wife. Why risk that?

In Betty's case, I would recommend that the nineteen-year-old find another place to live and the seventeen-year-old be put on notice. Even if Betty were to feel that she could hold out for one more year, I'd advise her to separate, since the children will blame her for having to move. Things could get a lot worse for her before they actually move, and that might be enough to destroy her feeling of love for Henry.

When the situation becomes unbearable for one spouse, they risk losing all their love for their husband or wife. Why risk that? It's best to simply separate for a while until both parents can live under the same roof in peace.

Meeting Intimate Needs in Mixed Families

This brings us to another problem that couples in mixed families face—they tend to lose their love for each other much quicker than most couples do. We've already discussed two reasons for this accelerated loss of love—failure to take each other's feelings into account when making parenting decisions, and stepchildren who make their lives miserable. Remember, whenever a couple feels bad when together, they're making Love Bank withdrawals. And mixed marriages can create a very unhappy environment.

But there's a third reason why mixed marriages do so badly—failure to meet intimate emotional needs. I've already warned you that those needs are much more difficult to meet after children arrive, and spouses in mixed marriages have children from the moment they marry.

I received the following letter from a husband dealing with this particular issue.

Dear Dr. Harley,

I suppose that I should have seen it coming, but I guess I was blinded by love. My friends warned me, but I wouldn't listen. They told me to watch out for Toni because she only wanted a man to support her family. They said she really didn't love me. Well, we've been married only three months, and I now know they were right.

Prior to marriage, Toni was very affectionate. Now she's stone cold. I'll file for divorce unless something changes quickly. What can I do to save our marriage?

Bert

It's unlikely that Toni married Bert just for his help raising her children. She probably loved him just as much as he loved her the day of their wedding. But whatever he did prior to marriage came to an abrupt halt after marriage. And it probably wasn't his fault.

As I've already mentioned, since all parents are protective of their own children, the Policy of Joint Agreement is particularly difficult to follow in mixed marriages. Failure to follow that policy leads to a very unpleasant home environment that causes massive Love Bank withdrawals. The parents are so protective of their children that they fail to protect each other.

But it's equally difficult to follow the Policy of Undivided Attention in mixed marriages. Prior to marriage, dates with-

Spouses in mixed marriages want to be with their children so often that they neglect time to be alone with each other.

out the children are common. Once married, however, spouses in mixed marriages want to be with their children as often as possible, and so they neglect time to be alone with each other. When they fail to spend time together, they also fail to make enough Love Bank deposits to sustain the feeling of love.

After merely three months of marriage, Toni was no longer in love with Bert. She'd been affectionate prior to marriage because she loved him, not because she wanted to hook him. And after she lost her love for him, she didn't feel like being affectionate anymore. Bert's accusations that she'd led him on probably made her angry, and his friends were certainly not helping the situation.

So how can Bert solve the problem? He should continue to meet Toni's intimate emotional needs as he had prior to marriage. Even though she's no longer in love with him and is very resentful about his accusations, there's still hope. If he can encourage her to follow the Policy of Undivided Attention for just one month, her love for him will likely be restored.

If I were counseling Toni, I'd encourage her to let Bert meet her intimate emotional needs and to try meeting his during that month. Although she's not accustomed to being affectionate toward someone she doesn't love, Bert is, after all, her husband—someone she promised to love and cherish. If she were to give him her undivided attention, eventually her feeling of love would return, and it would be much easier to care for him as he expects.

> In most mixed families, children have already suffered through one divorce. They don't need more trauma. They need to see an example of a healthy marriage.

Toni and Bert's experience is typical of most couples in mixed marriages. After marriage, they fail to create the privacy needed to meet each other's intimate emotional needs. And then, when the feelings of love are lost, instead of taking time to reestablish their romantic relationship, they cut each other off entirely.

Bert reacted the way most spouses do in this situation. "I'll file for divorce if something doesn't change quickly." And the vast majority of these couples do just that.

But what kind of a solution is that? In most mixed families, children have already suffered through one divorce. They don't need more trauma. They need parents to give both love and discipline, and they desperately need to see an example of a healthy marriage.

I'd be the first to admit that a romantic relationship is very difficult to sustain in a mixed marriage. But it can be done if you're willing to follow the Policy of Joint Agreement and the Policy of Undivided Attention. Those two rules will guarantee a romantic relationship in any marriage—even a mixed marriage!

Disorder or Gift?

How to Deal with ADHD

I was first introduced to Attention-Deficit/Hyperactivity Disorder (ADHD) in 1969. A friend of mine worked as a counselor at a juvenile detention center and was impressed by the fact that seventy percent of those incarcerated seemed to have these characteristics. It wasn't known as ADHD at the time, but what he described would eventually have that label.

He described the attention deficit part of the behavioral pattern as being easily distracted. The most common traits included failing to listen when spoken to, having difficulty organizing tasks and activities, being forgetful, having trouble following through on assignments, and losing things. Indicators of the hyperactive part included talking excessively, being "on the go," fidgeting and squirming in a chair, interrupting others, and having difficulty playing quietly.

A person didn't have to display these symptoms constantly to be labeled with this "disorder"; the symptoms only had to show up often. And school was where they would most often appear.

But the more I learned about these characteristics and how the disorder was related to juvenile delinquency, the more concerned I became. All those traits that were supposed to lead to a life of crime were also traits that *I'd* had throughout my childhood. In fact, I'm quite sure I've had them throughout my life, to a somewhat lesser extent.

But I'd never been in trouble with the law and I'd never even been in trouble at school. While I seemed to have much more energy than anyone else in my class and hated sitting still for more than ten minutes, it didn't get me into trouble. Instead, it helped me accomplish more than most other children could.

So when I first heard about the troubled youths diagnosed with ADHD, I was convinced that it wasn't the energy or even the distractibility that was getting them into trouble—it was their *thoughtlessness,* amplified by energy. They were unkind to others, and their high levels of energy made it apparent to all.

> ADHD children are like sports cars with high-horsepower V8 engines. Whatever they learn is magnified in their behavior.

Most boys in the juvenile detention center where my friend worked were from broken homes. They had been raised either by a single mother or by a remarried parent and a stepparent in a mixed family. The events leading to the divorce were certainly a poor example of how to get along in life; I would imagine that these children learned more about fighting from their parents than they learned about making peace. And when you added their high level of energy to their dysfunctional background, the resulting conduct became unbearable for everyone.

I've found ADHD children to be like sports cars with high-horsepower V8 engines. Whatever they learn is magnified in their behavior. If they learn to be demanding, disrespectful, and angry because their parents behave that way at home, they can become the scourge of a classroom.

On the other hand, if their parents teach them to be thoughtful, they can become the most caring children in school. It is important to remember that the way you behave will have a tremendous influence on your children. But the influence will be much more noticeable if your children are ADHD.

Bring on the Drugs

It wasn't long after my introduction to ADHD that I witnessed the advent of drugs to help prevent disruptive children from acting out in school. Instead of letting these children hold an entire class hostage with their thoughtless and inappropriate behavior, they were drugged. I was alarmed by that form of therapy since it did nothing to address the underlying cause of the problem—ineffective training at home.

But then the geniuses who decide what's good for children made a decision that was even more alarming—they decided to drug every child who was endowed with high energy. It was argued that children would learn more if they took these drugs. So instead of creating an educational climate that gave high-energy children a more appropriate learning environment, those in charge decided to relegate the kids to chairs all day and drug them so they would sit quietly.

By coming up with a diagnosis that made every high-energy child appear disabled, educators failed to recognize that high energy in children is a gift, not a disorder. That gift would be easy to demonstrate in an appropriate educational system. But the existing system catered to low-energy kids, those who would sit still all day at desks, quietly doing their work. It was a system

> High energy in children is a gift, not a disorder.

that drove high-energy children, like me, to *distraction,* so to speak. Instead of adjusting the system to help high-energy children excel, those in charge called those who had trouble adjusting to the existing system disabled. And then they drugged them so that they would conform to that system.

I was shocked at what I saw happening. I had firsthand experience with that flawed educational system because I'd gone through it myself. But it was before the diagnosis of ADHD and the subsequent administration of drugs, so I wasn't faced with drug therapy as I was growing up.

Your ADHD Child

Because so many children are diagnosed with ADHD, I've counseled many parents who are concerned about their children who have been given that label. But I draw a very important distinction between high-energy children who are thoughtless, and those who are thoughtful.

When high-energy children are also thoughtful, they can become some of the most caring people in your home. But children with the thoughtless variety of ADHD will wreak havoc in your household.

The following letter I received describes the typical problems of living with a thoughtless ADHD child.

Dear Dr. Harley,

I need some help with my marriage. I have read your book *Love Busters,* and it's been a big help to my wife, Rhonda, and I. However, I think I've discovered a new category of Love Buster, and I don't quite know how to deal with it. That Love Buster is my stepson, Brad. He suffers from Attention Deficit Hyperactive Disorder (ADHD), and it is really draining on my marriage. The heart of the problem is that my wife feels I don't treat our son fairly or show him enough love, and I, of course, think the opposite.

Dr. Harley, our son is a terror on two feet. He is only ten and he really wants to please us, but because of his handicap he does poorly in school, the dog does not get along with him, he is always breaking my wife's and my own personal belongings, and he steals from us. When I come home from work I never know what to expect. There is always bad news regarding something he's done. Since the bad news hurts me so much, I feel myself emotionally withdrawing from my son, and because I am withdrawn, my wife tells me that this is a Love Buster for her, and then she starts to withdraw from me. It's a vicious cycle.

We have tried support groups for ADHD and sought other counseling too, but so far it has not worked. I would greatly appreciate any advice that you can give me.

Richard

Reading between the lines, I assume that Rhonda wants Richard to react to her son's inconsiderate behavior with patience and love. She probably doesn't always react that way herself, but whenever she sees Richard upset with Brad, she feels as if he is upset with her. So she withdraws from him to escape the pain.

One approach to the problem is to count the years before Brad is out of the house. If their marriage can survive until he is old enough to leave, they can pick up the pieces and try to rebuild what their "Love Buster" almost destroyed.

> Children with the thoughtless variety of ADHD will raise havoc in a household.

But there's a better, proactive approach to this problem that will not only prevent the loss of love units but also guide Richard's stepson into a successful life. This approach has two parts, and both must be implemented if it is to work.

1. Make all child-training decisions together.

Richard and Rhonda should use the Policy of Joint Agreement whenever they make a child-training decision. They should begin by agreeing that from now on they will never discipline their son unless they can enthusiastically agree. No more mixed signals—Brad will be getting all of his reprimands from both of them or he won't get any at all. That means they will spend many hours discussing how to handle this "terror on two feet." But they'll do it together.

The Policy of Joint Agreement not only will help them overcome conflicts over discipline, but it will also set an example for their son. It's a rule that ensures thoughtfulness because it forces people to take each other's feelings into account.

Richard and Rhonda should consider the fact that Brad has high energy whenever they want to change his behavior. Asking him to "sit still" fails to recognize how painful it might be for him to fulfill this simple request. An alternative that allows him to burn some of his excess energy in a productive way yet avoids irritating those around him would be far more sensitive to his feelings.

Another important consideration in raising high-energy children is to avoid sugar in their diet. Sugar is a short-term energy booster, something these children don't need because they already have the energy of three kids. Most children like sugar-laden products, however, and it can be very difficult to tell them they can't have candy bars or a soda. But if you and your spouse agree to keep those products out of your child's hands, you'll go a long way toward helping him or her make successful adjustments to life.

> When you agree on a child-training strategy, you're more likely to succeed at channeling your child's energy.

It can be particularly difficult to know what's best for your high-energy child because of the "disability" label. It might make you think that your child needs therapy to overcome it. But if you can recognize your child's excessive energy as a gift and not a disability, you can help direct that energy into productive and socially acceptable activities. And when you and your spouse are in agreement about your child-training strategy, you're far more likely to succeed at channeling your child's energy.

2. Teach thoughtfulness with quality family time.

Richard and Rhonda must do more than just agree on how they will train Brad—they also must implement those decisions. And the best way to put their decisions into motion is to schedule quality family time each week. This time should be enjoyable for everyone—and educational for Brad. In fact, part of Brad's education should be learning how to make the time enjoyable for Richard and Rhonda as well as for himself.

Before each outing, Brad's opinions and preferences should be considered along with those of his parents. They should ask him to help plan the time so that all three of them will have fun. In the process of coming to an agreement, he will have to consider his parents' feelings just as much as they will have to consider his. They shouldn't go anywhere or do anything until they have an agreement from all three of them. And then while on the outing, just about everything they do should reflect their mutual thoughtfulness.

They should also plan ahead for their son's misbehavior so that it doesn't ruin their experiences together. One possibility is to give Brad an opportunity to burn excess energy if he starts to act up. Or if he becomes totally uncooperative, they should have contingency plans ready. Remember, this is an educational experience, and parents should expect mistakes.

But along with mistakes, Richard and Rhonda will also experience Brad's growth. The longer they have this time together as a family, the more enjoyable it will be for all of them because Brad will learn to be more thoughtful.

Richard and Rhonda have been failing to follow the Policy of Joint Agreement when it comes to raising their son, and I'm sure they are not spending much quality family time together. After all, Brad's behavior was so irritating to Richard that he wanted to avoid the child whenever possible.

But if their time together could be carefully planned to give Brad an opportunity to burn his excess energy and at the same time be influenced by his parents to be more thoughtful, eventually he will become someone whom Richard will thoroughly enjoy. And that's something Brad desperately needs.

Nature and Nurture

The amount of energy we have is essentially an inherited trait. But I've never been convinced that the factors leading to the thoughtless variety of high energy are inherited. There are so many similarities in the conditions under which thoughtless high-energy kids are raised that I believe environment plays a crucial role. My entire family is full of high-energy people. I could hardly sit still in school and even today find lectures almost intolerable. But I was trained to be considerate of others. My parents would not allow me to behave any other way.

My personal opinion is that thoughtless ADHD kids are not simply high-energy children—they are high-energy children who have not been taught to be thoughtful. What makes Brad a "Love Buster" isn't his high energy or his failure in school or his short attention span. It's his stealing, lying, disrespect, temper tantrums, abuse, and many other traits characteristic of those who've never been taught to be considerate. If Richard and Rhonda make a commitment to use the Policy of Joint Agreement in the way they train Brad, and spend quality family time together with an emphasis on cooperation and thoughtfulness, Brad's social problems will be solved.

> You and your spouse can't change nature. But that doesn't mean your high-energy child must run wild.

And once they've set aside time for their family, they'll find that the Policy of Joint Agreement will be much easier to implement. Rhonda will be happy to see Richard taking responsibility for her son's development and will want his influence to be effective. What had been a Love Buster will turn into a Love Builder. Richard's effort will not only deposit love units in her Love Bank but also help their son's selfish pattern of behavior begin to show signs of improvement.

Does this all sound too good to be true? If you're living with a thoughtless ADHD child, you may feel that nothing will bring peace to your home. But although you and your spouse can't change nature, you can adjust to your child's high energy. Of course, that doesn't mean your child has to run wild. High-energy children have a special gift, and if you train them through quality family time and the Policy of Joint Agreement, you can help them use their gift to benefit others instead of harming them.

14

When Grandma Won't Let Go
Dealing with Intrusive In-Laws

Sara and Larry were struggling with financial problems. They had just purchased a home for their new baby, Andrea, and their improved lifestyle was costing them far more than they'd anticipated. So Sara went back to work just six weeks after Andrea's birth.

But the cost of day care was much more than they had anticipated. They were both very discouraged after checking out a few centers nearby. With no other options, Larry asked Sara how she felt about leaving Andrea with his mother, Kate, while they were both at work. Under the circumstances, it seemed like a good idea to Sara. And Larry thought that his mom might also like the idea. She was having trouble adjusting to an empty home after her youngest daughter had gone to college.

When they introduced the plan to Kate, she was not just willing to take care of Andrea—she was overjoyed. It seemed to be the perfect solution for everyone. And for the first few weeks, everything went well.

But one Friday afternoon, Sara came by to pick up Andrea and happened to mention that they were taking her shopping that evening.

"Oh, you can't do that—Andrea has a cold and shouldn't be out in the night air," Kate warned.

"I think Andrea will be just fine," Sara responded. "We'll bundle her up."

"I can't let you take her if you'll be exposing her to the cold. Why don't you leave her here and come back later to pick her up," Kate suggested.

Quite frankly, it was a generous suggestion. It would give Sara and Larry an evening to themselves, and they needed the time together. But Sara took offense at the suggestion that she didn't know what would be good for her own daughter.

"Thanks for the offer, but we've been looking forward to having Andrea go out with us tonight," Sara said as she reached for the baby.

"I'm sorry, but I can't let you take her." Kate pulled Andrea away from the outreached arms of Sara, and the battle began.

"You will not be telling me how to raise my own child!" Sara screamed and snatched the crying Andrea right out of Kate's arms. As she rushed to the car, Kate followed and started calling Sara all sorts of names—a spoiled rotten wife and mother, among other things.

It was a disaster for both women. Sara went home and told Larry the whole story, demanding that they put Andrea into a day-care program immediately, whether or not they could afford it. Larry wanted to talk to his mother first, to get her side of the story, but his reluctance to support Sara made matters even worse. After he could see that she was not going to budge on the issue, he reluctantly agreed to go with her to look for another day-care option.

Kate was devastated. She had come to think of Andrea as her own daughter and was very emotionally attached to her. The very thought of losing the child during the day was unthinkable. By the time she had a chance to talk with Larry, she was almost irrational.

Kate and Sara eventually apologized to each other for their behavior, and Kate went back to taking care of Andrea again. But all of this hardship could have been easily avoided with the Policy of Joint Agreement.

When Mothers Meddle

Although most mothers have no desire to interfere with their children's marriages, all too often a mom will become embroiled in a power struggle with her son-in-law or daughter-in-law. With desperation as her motive, she usually feels guilty for the trouble she causes, but she can't think of an alternative because she's so emotionally affected by what goes on in her child's marriage.

> All too often a mom will become embroiled in a power struggle with her son-in-law or daughter-in-law.

There are numerous issues that can arise to get a reaction out of Mom—what church you attend, how you spend your money, where you choose to live, where you have lunch on Sunday, and a host of more trivial matters. But the problem is especially noticeable when a grandchild arrives. A grandmother often shares the protective instinct that a new mother feels for her child. And because of her experience raising children, she thinks she is in the best position to know what's good for the new baby.

You will undoubtedly have a conflict with your mother-in-law one day, if you have not had one already. It may not be as traumatic as the one Sara had with Kate, but regardless of the seriousness of the conflict, there's a way to resolve your problem that will minimize the damage.

So what could Sara have done differently? How could she have responded to her mother-in-law so that she did not have to relinquish control of her own daughter?

After Kate had warned, "Oh, you can't do that—Andrea has a cold and shouldn't be out in the night air," Sara would have been wise to say, "I appreciate your advice, and I'll discuss it with Larry when he comes home."

But Sara was not in the habit of using the Policy of Joint Agreement. Instead of waiting to make the final decision with her husband, she was in the habit of making independent decisions. So she made the unwise choice of announcing her verdict on the spot. In doing so, she not only aggravated the situation, but she also lost some of the clout she would've had with the support of her husband. If Kate had called the next day to find out if they'd taken Andrea shopping, they could have responded with a united front—they both had agreed to take the baby shopping.

Of course, that approach might've created a problem for Sara. Instead of agreeing with her to take Andrea shopping, Larry may have agreed with his mother that the baby was too sick to take out at night.

But if Sara had not yet expressed her opinion to Kate, saving face would not be at issue. Larry would be free to express his true opinion without fear of being considered unsupportive. So they could discuss the pros and cons of their plans for the evening and arrive at an intelligent solution to the problem. After respectfully discussing the alternatives with each other, they could have decided to bring Andrea back to Kate and enjoy the evening out by themselves. Or they could have decided to stay home that night to be with Andrea. But whatever the final outcome, they would have respected each other's feelings and opinions.

Without a doubt, Sara's interests should be more important to Larry than his mother's interests. But the Policy of Joint Agreement protects Sara's interests, even if Larry agrees with his mother. It doesn't allow them to do anything with Andrea unless Sara enthusiastically agrees to it. If she were to decide that it was unhealthy for Kate to be caring for Andrea so much, she would have the right to pull the plug. And she wouldn't have to give any more of an explanation than that it was making her feel uncomfortable.

The Policy of Joint Agreement forces both spouses to put each other first in all decisions. But Larry would not be completely abandoning his mother's interests by following the policy. It's just that her interests would be considered in a way that didn't conflict with Sara's interests.

The Dependent In-Law

Over the centuries, mothers-in-law have been given a bad rap. Because of a few who are insensitive or misunderstood, they're all often viewed with suspicion. The facts don't support the bias, however. In the vast majority of cases, mothers-in-law, my own included, are terrific.

However, from time to time, an otherwise terrific mother-in-law can become terrible when her husband dies, leaving her to depend on her children for survival. Sandy wrote me for my perspective on this problem.

Dear Dr. Harley,

I've been married for three years to a man whose mother has almost no life outside of him. She is totally devoted to Alan to the exclusion of just about everything—work, hobbies, and friends. Plus, she turns to him for advice on everything from programming the VCR to complex legal transactions. He is an only child whose father left before he was born.

In the early part of our relationship, about seven years ago, his grandfather, who raised him for a good portion of his childhood, was very ill. Consequently, his mother called quite frequently, and I didn't think too much of it considering the circumstances.

When my husband's grandfather passed away, his mother inherited quite a bit of money. Free of financial pressures, she had (and still has) the opportunity to do just about anything she wants. Instead, she has become increasingly involved in my husband's life and mine, too, by association.

Meanwhile, I have felt more and more encroached upon.

I, obviously, have handled the situation badly, because our disagreements over her role in his life have deepened. He has always defended her actions and now I'm told that the things that transpire between the two of them are none of my business.

I have often wished she would go get a life and have made several suggestions. But she has told me that school is boring, work is boring, traveling used to be okay but is now boring, even people her own age (late fifties) are boring.

My husband and I had planned on having children, but I refuse to start a family with so many intrusions from his mother. In fact, lately I've been considering leaving my husband. What should I do?

Sandy

When a woman loses her husband through death or divorce, she often finds herself quite alone in the world. Instinctively, she turns to her children for emotional support. Although she often has no desire to interfere with their marriages, she can become embroiled in a power struggle with her son-in-law or daughter-in-law, who sees her as a nuisance at best and a threat at worst.

Sandy's mother-in-law has become increasingly dependent on her son, Alan, and thinks she cannot live without him. He's the most important person in her life, and her desperation may prevent her from seeing the situation objectively. In fact, she may have already talked to her son about how important he is to her and how she couldn't live without him.

Most people feel they owe a great deal to their mothers, who gave birth to them and raised them. So when their mother asks for help, they feel obliged to come to the rescue. Their spouse is also important to them, but they feel their spouse should encourage them to help their mother—not discourage them. They often view protests as self-centered jealousy rather than legitimate complaints.

This is one of those situations that requires the wisdom of Solomon. On the one hand, there are the needs of a desperate mother with no one to turn to except her son, and on the other hand, there are the needs of a wife who finds her mother-in-law's intrusions threatening. It is for these very situations that the Policy of Joint Agreement was written. The policy helps decide what to do when there are no easy answers.

In this case, Alan is trying to decide between Sandy's interests and the interests of his mother. Which are more important? Of course, he wants to please them both. But lately, he's been ignoring Sandy's feelings because he thinks his mother is in a more desperate situation. That choice has motivated Sandy to consider leaving him.

If Alan wants a decent marriage, he must learn to put his wife's interests before all others, even those of his own mother. It means that whatever he does for his mother *must* be with Sandy's enthusiastic agreement or he should not do it. Sandy must approve every act of care he wants to give to his mother, or to anyone else for that matter.

> You don't need to abandon your mother to please your spouse— just consider your spouse's interests first.

For example, suppose Alan's mother calls at 7:30 in the evening wanting to talk to him about something. He should first ask how Sandy feels about taking time out of their evening together to talk to his mother. Sandy may agree to his conversation with her as long as it's no longer than ten minutes. He should then respect her feelings by watching the clock and ending the conversation within the ten minutes.

Since handling his mother's finances is part of his care for her, Alan should tell Sandy precisely what they discuss together. Everything that goes on in his life is Sandy's business, and she should know about as much of it as possible. She may need to know how their planning might affect her, especially in regard to such things as his inheritance.

If the Policy of Joint Agreement is not followed, Sandy's problem will get worse over time. Even if her mother-in-law passes away, she will always remember that Alan put his mother's feelings above her own. But if the policy is followed, it's unlikely that Alan will feel guilty or resentful for having failed his mother. It doesn't require abandonment of his mother to please his wife. Instead, it simply guides him toward ways of helping his mother that are sensitive to his wife's interests.

Burning Bridges

While some mothers-in-law are innocent victims of their own desperation, others simply don't deserve the care they crave. Sally found herself in a situation in which her husband had to make a choice—it was either Sally or his mother.

Dear Dr. Harley,

My husband, Harold, and I have just split up. The only problem in our marriage was his mother. She has made comments suggesting that I have kidnapped her son; I've taken him away from his family. And she has just recently taken a fondness to calling me lewd names. The big problem for me is not so much those comments (I try to consider the source of one that would do such things) but that my husband sticks up for her. Part of the problem is that my mother-in-law's husband is an alcoholic and she has always looked to her son for help.

Yesterday when we were arguing she happened to call. Sensing he was upset, they (both his parents) drove over and tried to "rescue" him (as if I had him locked up or something). Well, suffice it to say, there was quite the scene (she called me a tramp and a whore, etc.) and I asked Harold to leave afterwards.

I just really got tired of feeling that if his mother and I were both drowning, she'd get the life preserver. I'm not saying I'm an angel in all of this. Far from it, I'm sure. I've antagonized her, but that was after she said insulting things about me. Well, given all of this, I wonder if you think that we are way past counseling. I feel as if we are, but I'd really appreciate your opinion.

Sally

Sally's mother-in-law is not the "only problem" in her marriage. When she mentioned in her letter that she and her husband, Harold, were arguing, she tipped me off to the fact that they have other problems too. If they argue—perhaps fight—it's because they have not learned how to negotiate successfully. It's no surprise that their arguing hasn't solved their mother-in-law problem, and it's likely that other problems are also unresolved.

If Sally and Harold were to resolve their conflicts by taking each other's interests into account, they wouldn't argue—and they certainly wouldn't fight. There would be no reason for his parents to come over to "rescue" him. If they were following the Policy of Joint Agreement and the Four Steps to Successful Negotiation, these problems with Sally's in-laws, and all other problems for that matter, would eventually be resolved.

But what can you do with in-laws who are rude? What if Sally were not arguing with Harold, and her mother-in-law still called her names? The Policy of Joint Agreement solves that problem, too.

In-laws can burn their bridges. Unless Sally's mother-in-law treats her with courtesy and respect, Sally has the right to blackball her. The Policy of Joint Agreement makes Sally's feelings so important that if Harold's parents want to see him regularly, they must treat Sally as one of their own. If they don't, they may not be able to visit either Sally or their son.

> The Policy of Joint Agreement can put your marriage and your relationship with the in-laws back on solid ground.

Harold must put Sally's interests first if he wants a fulfilling marriage. That may mean cutting off his relationship with his mother, at least until she shows Sally the respect she deserves. When you marry, you should protect your spouse from your own destructive instincts, and in some cases, from those of your mother.

In the final analysis, in-laws should treat their children's spouses with utmost care. It's in their child's best interest, in their child's spouse's best interest, and even in their own best interest to keep their relationship respectful. But if your in-laws aren't acting appropriately and it's been threatening your love for your spouse, it's time to start applying the Policy of Joint Agreement. It can put your marriage and your relationship with the in-laws back on solid ground.

Setting a Healthy Example

Good in-law relationships do more than help a marriage—they also set a good example for children and allow them to enjoy a better relationship with their grandparents. Granted, there are in-laws who create so much trouble that a complete separation from them may be the only answer. But in the vast majority of cases, thoughtful negotiation solves the problem. And when parents solve their in-law problems using the Policy of Joint Agreement, it teaches children a very important lesson about problem-solving—and about marriage.

But most important, by solving disagreements about in-laws with joint agreement, you and your spouse protect your love for each other. And that gives children what they need the most—parents who are in love.

Love Is Fragile, Handle with Care

For Lovers Who Are Parents

As husbands and wives embark on the journey of parenthood, few imagine that their own children could cause their marriage to crash and burn. But all too often, that's exactly what happens. The love-struck couple who couldn't keep their eyes off each other on their wedding day eventually find themselves too busy to even look at each other. That's because they spend so much of their time caring for their children that there's none left to care for each other.

Has this happened to you? Do you find yourselves so busy that you have no time to give each other the care you need? If so, this book was written for you, and I hope I've convinced you that it's time to make some changes. Maintaining your love for each other during the parenting years is essential to the health of your marriage. And as we've seen, the survival of your marriage is essential to the health of your children.

Doing what it takes to sustain your romantic relationship makes you good parents. But a romantic relationship does more for your children than just preventing your divorce. It also sets an example on how to be successful in life. To sustain your love while raising children, you must meet each other's intimate emotional needs, avoid hurting each other, and make lifestyle decisions that take each other's feelings into account. Putting these principles into practice in your marriage sets an example for children that no amount of teaching can replace.

And that's been a recurring theme of this book—children learn by example. If you want your children to keep their rooms clean, keep your own room clean. If you want your children to do their homework, fulfill your own responsibilities. If you want your children to avoid arguing and fighting, avoid arguing and fighting with each other. But most importantly, if you want your children to grow up to be thoughtful of others, you must be thoughtful of each other.

Romantic Love Is Fragile

Romantic love is the feeling of incredible attraction to someone of the opposite sex. When you have that feeling for someone who is also in love with you, you're on top of the world. In fact, it's such a great feeling that people are willing to do almost anything to sustain it—even marry the person.

Marriage doesn't guarantee romantic love.

But as most couples soon find out, marriage itself doesn't guarantee romantic love. The emotional needs that were met so well during dating are rarely met consistently after marriage. Instead, spouses usually neglect each other, especially after children arrive. And then they wake up one day realizing that what made them feel so attracted to each other has escaped them. When that feeling is gone, the marriage itself is threatened.

Romantic love may be fragile, but it can be sustained throughout your marriage. When a fragile object is shipped in the mail, it usually carries the label "handle with care." If the handlers follow the advice on the label, the package gets to its destination in perfect condition. And that's exactly what you'll need to do to stay in love. All it takes is following a few rules that not only guarantee romantic love but also help children grow to be happy and successful.

Rule #1: Meet each other's intimate emotional needs.

I've defined a romantic relationship as two people in love who meet each other's intimate emotional needs—intimate affection, intimate conversation, sexual fulfillment, and recreational companionship. When these needs are met, they deposit so many love units that they tend to trigger the feeling of romantic love.

Quite frankly, if almost any two people of the opposite sex meet any of these needs for each other, they'll usually be in love before long. That's why affairs often get started very innocently. If you share some of your deepest thoughts and feelings with someone of the opposite sex at work (intimate conversation), express your care for each other (intimate affection), and spend some of your most enjoyable rec-reational time with that person (recreational companionship), you will almost always desire sexual fulfillment with that person. We're all wired for romantic relationships, and when our needs are met, whether it's by our spouse or someone else, we fall in love with that person.

> Meeting intimate emotional needs triggers the feeling of romantic love.

In marriage, if these needs are met con-sistently, a romantic relationship is sus-tained and all is well with the world. But if these needs are not met, we not only lose the feeling of love, but we also become vulnerable to anyone outside of marriage who meets them for us. That's why affairs are so common and threaten marriages so much.

Your most heartfelt affection, intimate conversation, recreational companionship, and sexual fulfillment should be met *exclusively* in marriage. Once married, your most fulfilling conversations should be with each other, your deepest expressions of love should be for each other, your favorite recreational activities should be with each other, and your complete sexual fulfillment should be with each other. That's an extremely important lesson for children, because it will not only help them create a fulfilling marriage for themselves when they become adults, but it will also help them understand why their parents need to be alone so much of the time.

Children should understand that intimate emotional needs are best met in private. While they may observe some of the affection and intimate conversation that parents who are lovers express in public, they can only guess at what is going on in private. So they should be told what's going on and why. Otherwise, it will appear as if their parents don't care about them.

The Policy of Undivided Attention is designed to help spouses schedule time each week to meet each other's intimate emotional needs. In our busy lives, we are tempted to let lower priorities crowd out higher priorities. So deliberate scheduling of fifteen hours each week for undivided attention gets our priorities straight. Your marriage will not be worth much without a romantic relationship, and unless you schedule enough time for it, it won't happen.

Truth is, parents who care most about their children will guard their romantic relationship. That's because so much of their care for their children depends on it.

Rule #2: Avoid hurting each other.

One of the saddest aspects of being a marriage counselor is witnessing the suffering spouses inflict on each other. Marriage should be a relationship of extraordinary care and protection, yet for many it becomes unbearable. Whenever I argue that divorce is very destructive for children, a common response is that the abuse they witness at home is also destructive. Divorce gives children an escape from relentless arguing and fighting.

But there's another escape from abuse that doesn't require divorce: Stop the fighting. Instead of setting a bad example for children by creating an unsafe environment, give children a good example of how to solve problems without the Love Busters of selfish demands, disrespectful judgments, and angry outbursts. Any couple can learn to end abuse once and for all, and when they achieve this objective, their children benefit.

Dishonesty in marriage is a Love Buster that destroys trust between spouses. It's impossible to sustain a romantic relationship if you lie to each other. And dishonesty sets a very bad example for children. If you want your children to tell the truth, you must tell each other the truth.

> Any couple can learn to end abuse once and for all.

You also must learn to avoid annoying habits that deplete Love Bank balances. Children can be very annoying at times and need to learn how to become more considerate of those around them. But how can they learn to be considerate when the annoying habits of their parents go on unabated? When you or your spouse claims, "It's just the way I am," shouldn't a child be able to claim the same excuse? Annoying habits show thoughtlessness toward others, and parents should eliminate them as an example for their children.

Don't hurt each other with independent behavior either. Almost everything you do affects your spouse, and if you behave as if your spouse doesn't exist, the pain you inflict can be overwhelming. You must recognize each other's existence in every aspect of your lives by making all your decisions with each other's interests in mind. Mutually agreeable decisions are a key ingredient in your love for each other. And they're also a key ingredient in a successful relationship with others. We all depend on other people for our survival—none of us is independent. And that's one of the most important lessons your children should learn.

Rule #3: Create a lifestyle that's enjoyable for both of you.

Marriage is a team sport—it requires the cooperation of both players. One spouse can't play the game as if the other doesn't exist and expect to win. Similarly, the lifestyle created in marriage should be a cooperative effort that benefits both spouses. Otherwise, it will turn out to be mutually unfulfilling.

I've written the Policy of Joint Agreement to help couples achieve a compatible lifestyle. *Never do anything without an enthusiastic agreement between you and your spouse.* While it's tempting to make decisions that benefit you at the expense of your spouse, this policy prevents you from acting on those destructive temptations. If the policy is strictly followed for just one year, the most incompatible couple will become compatible again.

> Marriage is a team sport—it requires the cooperation of both players.

Before you make any lifestyle decisions, ask your spouse how he or she would feel about it. If there's enthusiastic agreement, go for it. If not, go back to the drawing board. This simple policy will build thoughtfulness into your relationship.

Children also need to learn the importance of thoughtfulness. Your example will help them see that they don't live in a vacuum but are surrounded by people who are affected by what they do. And by watching you follow the Policy of Joint Agreement, they'll learn how to ask others about their feelings; and they'll try to achieve their objectives with the interests of others in mind.

I believe the value of thoughtfulness is one of the most important values you can teach your children. When they think about others before they act, it helps them avoid most of the problems they could experience as adults. And they'll be much easier to raise if they consider the feelings of their parents too.

One of the best ways to teach thoughtfulness is to give them fifteen hours a week of quality family time: That time with your children will not only help them learn to consider the feelings of others, it will also meet a very important emotional need for your spouse—the need for family commitment.

Handle with Care

Would you place an expensive antique vase in the middle of a
hallway, where people could easily walk into it and knock it over? Of
course not. You'd set it in a place that would provide protection—perhaps a glass cabinet.

Unfortunately, many couples treat their love with less care than
they do valuable objects. They shove it aside or hammer away at it.
When they stop caring for each other and stop protecting each other
from their selfish instincts, their love eventually shatters. And then
their children are forced to deal with the trauma of divorce.

Your love is extremely valuable to you and your children. But it's
also very fragile. So give it the protection it deserves by following my
three rules: (1) Meet each other's emotional needs, (2) avoid hurting each other, and (3) create a lifestyle that's enjoyable for both of
you. If you and your spouse put these three rules into action, your
relationship will be safe and secure.

What helps parents stay in love with each other also helps parents
raise happy and successful children. And that's good news for you,
because it means that doing what it takes to sustain your romantic
relationship will also make you great parents.

The Most Important Emotional Needs

Affection

Quite simply, affection is the expression of love. It symbolizes security, protection, comfort, and approval—vitally important ingredients in any relationship. When one spouse is affectionate to the other, the following messages are sent:

1. You are important to me, and I will care for you and protect you.
2. I'm concerned about the problems you face and will be there for you when you need me.

A hug can say those things. When we hug our friends and relatives, we are demonstrating our care for them. And there are other ways to show our affection—a greeting card, an "I love you" note, a bouquet of flowers, holding hands, walks after dinner, back rubs, phone calls, and conversations with thoughtful and loving expressions can all communicate affection.

Affection is, for many, the essential cement of a relationship. Without it many people feel totally alienated. With it they become emotionally bonded. If you feel terrific when your spouse is affectionate and you feel terrible when there is not enough affection, you have the emotional need for affection.

Sexual Fulfillment

We often confuse sex and affection. Affection is an act of love that is nonsexual and can be received from friends, relatives, children, and even pets. However, acts that can show affection, such as hugging and kissing, that are done with a sexual motive are actually sex, not affection.

Most people know whether or not they have a need for sex, but in case there is any uncertainty, I will point out some of the most obvious symptoms.

A sexual need usually predates your current relationship and is somewhat independent of your relationship. While you may have discovered a deep desire to make love to your spouse since you've been in love, it isn't quite the same thing as a sexual need. Wanting to make love when you are in love is sometimes merely a reflection of wanting to be emotionally and physically close.

Sexual fantasies are usually a dead giveaway for a sexual need. Fantasies in general are good indicators of emotional needs—your most common fantasies usually reflecting your most important needs. If you have imagined what it would be like having your sexual need met in the most fulfilling ways, you probably have a sexual need. The more the fantasy is employed, the greater your need. And the way your sexual need is met in your fantasy is usually a good indicator of your sexual predispositions and orientation.

When you married, you and your spouse both promised to be faithful to each other for life. This means that you agreed to be each other's only sexual partner "until death do us part." You made this commitment because you trusted each other to meet your sexual needs, to be sexually available and responsive. The need for sex, then, is a very exclusive need, and if you have it, you will be very dependent on your spouse to meet it for you. You have no other ethical choice.

Conversation

Unlike sex, conversation is not a need that can be met exclusively in marriage. Our need for conversation can be ethically met by almost anyone. But if it is one of your most important emotional needs, whoever meets it best will deposit so many love units, you may fall in love with that person. So if it's your need, be sure that your spouse is the one who meets it the best and most often.

Men and women don't have too much difficulty talking to each other during courtship. That's a time of information gathering for both partners. Both are highly motivated to discover each other's likes and dislikes, personal background, current interests, and plans for the future.

But after marriage many women find that the man who would spend hours talking to her on the telephone now seems to have lost all interest in talking to her and spends his spare time watching television or reading. If your need for conversation was fulfilled during courtship, you expect it to be met after marriage.

If you see conversation as a practical necessity, primarily as a means to an end, you probably don't have much of a need for it. But if you have a craving just to talk to someone, if you pick up the telephone just because you feel like talking, if you enjoy conversation in its own right, consider conversation to be one of your most important emotional needs.

Recreational Companionship

A need for recreational companionship combines two needs into one: the need to engage in recreational activities and the need to have a companion.

During your courtship, you and your spouse were probably each other's favorite recreational companions. It's not uncommon for women to join men in hunting, fishing, watching football, or other activities they would never choose on their own. They simply want to spend as much time as possible with the man they like, and that means going where he goes.

The same is true of men. Shopping centers are not unfamiliar to men in love. They will also take their dates out to dinner, watch romantic movies, and attend concerts and plays. They take every opportunity to be with someone they like and try to enjoy the activity to guarantee more dates in the future.

I won't deny that marriage changes a relationship considerably. But does it have to end the activities that helped make the relationship so compatible? Can't a husband's favorite recreational companion be his wife and vice versa?

If recreational activities are important to you and you like to have someone join you for them to be fulfilling, include recreational companionship on your list of needs. Think about it for a moment in terms of the Love Bank. How much do you enjoy these activities and how many love units would your spouse be depositing whenever you enjoyed them together? What a waste it would be if someone else got credit for all those love units! And if it is someone of the opposite sex, it would be downright dangerous.

Who should get credit for all those love units? The one you should love the most, your spouse. That's precisely why I encourage a husband and wife to be each other's favorite recreational companion. It's one of the simplest ways to deposit love units.

Honesty and Openness

Most of us want an honest relationship with our spouse. But some of us have a need for such a relationship because honesty and openness give us a sense of security.

To feel secure, we want accurate information about our spouse's thoughts, feelings, habits, likes, dislikes, personal history, daily activities, and plans for the future. If a spouse does not provide honest and open communication, trust can be undermined and the feelings of security can eventually be destroyed. We can't trust the signals that are being sent and we have no foundation on which to build a solid relationship. Instead of adjusting to each other, we feel off balance; instead of growing together, we grow apart.

Aside from the practical considerations of honesty and openness, there are some of us who feel happy and fulfilled when our spouse reveals his or her most private thoughts to us. And we feel very frustrated when they are hidden. That reaction is evidence of an emotional need, one that can and should be met in marriage.

An Attractive Spouse

For many people, physical appearance can become one of the greatest sources of love units. If you have this need, an attractive person will not only get your attention, but may distract you from whatever you're doing. In fact, that's what may have first drawn you to your spouse—his or her physical appearance.

There are some who consider this need to be temporary and important only in the beginning of a relationship. After a couple get to know each other better, some feel that physical attractiveness should take a backseat to deeper and more intimate needs.

But that's not been my experience, nor has it been the experience of many people whom I've counseled, particularly men. For many, the need for an attractive spouse continues on throughout marriage, and just seeing the spouse looking attractive deposits love units.

Among the various aspects of physical attractiveness, weight generally gets the most attention. However, choice of clothing, hairstyle, makeup, and personal hygiene also come together to make a person attractive. It can be very subjective, and you are the judge of what is attractive to you.

If the attractiveness of your spouse makes you feel great, and loss of that attractiveness would make you feel very frustrated, you should probably include this category on your list of important emotional needs.

Financial Support

People often marry for the financial security that their spouse provides them. In other words, part of the reason they marry is for money. Is financial support one of your important emotional needs?

It may be difficult for you to know how much you need financial support, especially if your spouse has always been gainfully employed. But what if, before marriage, your spouse had told you not to expect any income from him or her? Would it have affected your decision to marry? Or what if your spouse could not find work, and you had to financially support him or her throughout life? Would that withdraw love units?

You may have a need for financial support if you expect your spouse to earn a living. But you definitely have that need if you do not expect to be earning a living yourself, at least during part of your marriage.

What constitutes financial support? Earning enough to buy everything you could possibly desire or earning just enough to get by? Different couples would answer this differently, and the same couples might answer differently in different stages of life. But like many of these emotional needs, financial support is sometimes hard to talk about. As a result, many couples have hidden expectations, assumptions, and resentments. Try to understand what you expect from your spouse financially to feel fulfilled. And what would it take for you to feel frustrated? Your analysis will help you determine if you have a need for financial support.

Domestic Support

The need for domestic support is a time bomb. At first it seems irrelevant, a throwback to more primitive times. But for many couples, the need explodes after a few years of marriage, surprising both husband and wife.

Domestic support includes cooking meals, washing dishes, washing and ironing clothes, cleaning house, and caring for children. If you feel very fulfilled when your spouse does these things and very annoyed when they are not done, you have the need for domestic support.

In earlier generations, it was assumed that all husbands had this need and all wives would naturally meet it. Times have changed, and needs have changed along with them. Now many of the men I counsel would rather have their wives meet their needs for affection or conversation, needs that have traditionally been more characteristic of women. And many women, especially career women, gain a great deal of pleasure having their husbands create a peaceful and well-managed home environment.

Marriage usually begins with a willingness of both spouses to share domestic responsibilities. Newlyweds commonly wash dishes together, make the bed together, and divide many household tasks. The groom welcomes his wife's help in doing what he had to do by himself as a bachelor. At this point in marriage, neither of them would identify domestic support as an important emotional need. But the time bomb is ticking.

When does the need for domestic support explode? When the children arrive! Children create huge needs—both a greater need for income and greater domestic responsibilities. The previous division of labor becomes obsolete. Both spouses must take on new responsibilities—and which ones will they take?

At this point in your marriage, you may find no need for domestic support at all. But that may change later when you have children. In fact, as soon as you are expecting your first child, you will find yourselves dramatically changing your priorities.

Family Commitment

In addition to a greater need for income and domestic responsibilities, the arrival of children creates in many people the need for family commitment. Again, if you don't have children yet, you may not sense this need, but when the first child arrives, a change may take place that you didn't anticipate.

Family commitment is not just child care—feeding, clothing, or watching over children to keep them safe. Child care falls under the category of domestic support. Family commitment, on the other hand, is a responsibility for the development of the children, teaching them the values of cooperation and care for each other. It is spending quality time with your children to help them develop into successful adults.

Evidence of this need is a craving for your spouse's involvement in the educational and moral development of your children. When he or she is helping care for them, you feel very fulfilled, and when he or she neglects their development, you feel very frustrated.

We all want our children to be successful, but if you have the need for family commitment, your spouse's participation in family activities will deposit carloads of love units. And your spouse's neglect of your children will noticeably withdraw them.

Admiration

If you have the need for admiration, you may have fallen in love with your spouse partly because of his or her compliments to you. Some people just love to be told that they are appreciated. Your spouse also may have been careful not to criticize you. If you have a need for admiration, criticism may hurt you deeply.

Many of us have a deep desire to be respected, valued, and appreciated by our spouse. We need to be affirmed clearly and often. There's nothing wrong with feeling that way. Even God wants us to appreciate him!

Appreciation is one of the easiest needs to meet. Just a compliment, and presto, you've made your spouse's day. On the other hand, it's also easy to be critical. A trivial word of rebuke can be very upsetting

to some people, ruining their day and withdrawing love units at an
alarming rate.

Your spouse may have the power to build up or deplete his or her
account in your Love Bank with just a few words. If you can be affected
that easily, be sure to add admiration to your list of important emotional
needs.

Time for Undivided Attention Work Sheet

(copy and enlarge this work sheet before use)

For the Week of _____

Please report the time you give undivided attention to each other. You must be without friends, relatives, or children and must use the time to engage in conversation, affection, sex, or recreational activities that promote undivided attention.

First, schedule time to be together by completing the Planned Time Together part of this report. The total for the week should add up to fifteen hours or more. Then, as the week unfolds, complete the Actual Time Together part of the report. The estimate of time actually given to undivided attention depends on how each of you feels about the attention given. While you may have been together for two hours, one of you may feel only half of the time was given to undivided attention, while the other may feel that the entire two hours qualified. Because of this common difference of opinion, each of you is to provide your own estimate. In the last column, the lower estimate is to be entered. If the planned activity was canceled, explain why under Actual Activities.

At the end of the week, the total of the Lower Estimate column should be entered on the Time for Undivided Attention Graph. It should be fifteen hours or more if you want to sustain romantic love in your marriage.

Planned Time Together

Planned Date	Planned Time (from–to)	Total Planned Time	Planned Activities
Total Time for the Week		_____	

Actual Time Together

Actual Activities	Her Estimate	His Estimate	Lower Estimate
Total Time for the Week			_____

Time for Undivided Attention Graph

(copy and enlarge this graph before use)

Hours of Undivided Attention

30

25

20

15

10

5

0   1   2   3   4   5   6   7   8   9   10   11   12   13   14   15   16   17   18   19   20   21   22   23   24   25   26

Index

Willard F. Harley, Jr., Ph.D., is a clinical psychologist and marriage counselor. Over the past twenty-five years he has helped thousands of couples overcome marital conflict and restore their love for each other. His innovative counseling methods are described in the books and articles he writes. *His Needs, Her Needs* has been a best seller since it was published in 1986 and has been translated into German, French, Dutch, and Chinese. Dr. Harley also leads training workshops for couples and marriage counselors and has appeared on hundreds of radio and television programs.

Willard Harley and Joyce, his wife of forty-two years, live in White Bear Lake, Minnesota. They are the parents of two married children who are also marriage counselors.

Dr. Harley would be delighted to hear from you. His website is
http://www.marriagebuilders.com

WANT TO ADD EVEN MORE *sizzle* TO YOUR MARRIAGE?

In this best-selling book, Dr. Willard F. Harley, Jr., identifies the ten most vital needs of women and men and shows husbands and wives how to satisfy those needs in their spouses. He provides guidance for becoming irresistible to your spouse and for loving more creatively and sensitively, thereby eliminating the problems that often lead to extramarital affairs.

Unabridged audio
360 minutes

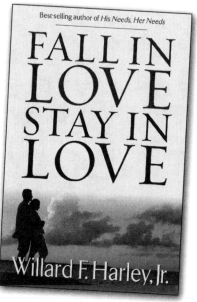
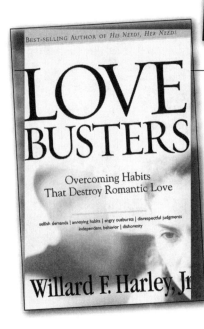

A helpful workbook containing all the contracts, questionnaires, inventories, and worksheets Dr. Harley recommends in *Love Busters* and *His Needs, Her Needs.*

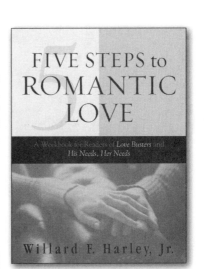

Give others the knowledge to build a lifelong, romantic love! *I Cherish You* highlights the concepts of *His Needs, Her Needs* in a beautiful gift format—perfect for celebrating a wedding or anniversary, or just to say "I love you."

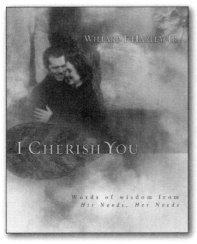

A guide to understanding and surviving every aspect of infidelity—from the beginning of an affair through the restoration of a marriage.

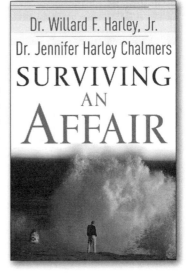

MARRIAGE BUILDERS®

Building Marriages To Last A Lifetime

Dr. Harley has saved thousands of marriages from the pain of unresolved conflict and the disaster of divorce. His successful approach to building marriages can help you too.

Why do people fall in love? Why do they fall out of love? What do they want most in marriage? What drives them out of marriage? How can a bad marriage become a great marriage? Dr. Harley's basic concepts address these and other important aspects of marriage building.

At www.marriagebuilders.com Dr. Harley introduces visitors to some of the best ways to overcome marital conflicts and some of the quickest ways to restore love. From the pages of "Basic Concepts" and articles by Dr. Harley to the archives for his weekly Q&A columns and information about upcoming seminars, this site is packed with useful material.

Let Marriage Builders™ help you build a marriage to last a lifetime!
www.marriagebuilders.com